D1084722

Eminem

Eminem

By Christie Brewer Boyd

LUCENT BOOKS
A part of Gale, Cengage Learning

GALE
CENGAGE Learning·

Detroit • New York • San Francisco • New Haven, Conn • Waterville, Maine • London

© 2012 Gale, Cengage Learning

LIBRARY OF CONGRESS CATALOGING-IN-PUBLICATION DATA

Boyd, Christie Brewer.
　Eminem / by Christie Brewer Boyd.
　　p. cm. -- (People in the news)
　Includes bibliographical references and index.
　ISBN 978-1-4205-0753-9 (hardcover)
　1. Eminem (Musician)--Juvenile literature. 2. Rap musicians--United States--Biography--Juvenile literature. I. Title.
　　ML3930.E46B69 2012
　　782.421649092--dc23
　　[B]

2012003266

Lucent Books
27500 Drake Rd
Farmington Hills MI 48331

ISBN-13: 978-1-4205-0753-9
ISBN-10: 1-4205-0753-2

Printed in the United States of America
1 2 3 4 5 6 7 16 15 14 13 12

Contents

Foreword

Fame and celebrity are alluring. People are drawn to those who walk in fame's spotlight, whether they are known for great accomplishments or for notorious deeds. The lives of the famous pique public interest and attract attention, perhaps because their experiences seem in some ways so different from, yet in other ways so similar to, our own.

Newspapers, magazines, and television regularly capitalize on this fascination with celebrity by running profiles of famous people. For example, television programs such as *Entertainment Tonight* devote all their programming to stories about entertainment and entertainers. Magazines such as *People* fill their pages with stories of the private lives of famous people. Even newspapers, newsmagazines, and television news frequently delve into the lives of well-known personalities. Despite the number of articles and programs, few provide more than a superficial glimpse at their subjects.

Lucent's People in the News series offers young readers a deeper look into the lives of today's newsmakers, the influences that have shaped them, and the impact they have had in their fields of endeavor and on other people's lives. The subjects of the series hail from many disciplines and walks of life. They include authors, musicians, athletes, political leaders, entertainers, entrepreneurs, and others who have made a mark on modern life and who, in many cases, will continue to do so for years to come.

These biographies are more than factual chronicles. Each book emphasizes the contributions, accomplishments, or deeds that have brought fame or notoriety to the individual and shows how that person has influenced modern life. Authors portray their subjects in a realistic, unsentimental light. For example, Bill Gates—the cofounder and former chief executive officer of the software giant Microsoft—has been instrumental in making personal computers the most vital tool of the modern age. Few dispute his business savvy, his perseverance, or his technical expertise, yet critics say he is ruthless in his dealings with competitors and driven more by his desire to maintain Microsoft's dominance in the computer industry than by an interest in furthering technology.

In these books, young readers will encounter inspiring stories about real people who achieved success despite enormous obstacles. Oprah Winfrey—one of the most powerful, most watched, and wealthiest women in television history—spent the first six years of her life in the care of her grandparents while her unwed mother sought work and a better life elsewhere. Her adolescence was colored by pregnancy at age fourteen, rape, and sexual abuse.

Each author documents and supports his or her work with an array of primary and secondary source quotations taken from diaries, letters, speeches, and interviews. All quotes are footnoted to show readers exactly how and where biographers derive their information and provide guidance for further research. The quotations enliven the text by giving readers eyewitness views of the life and accomplishments of each person covered in the People in the News series.

In addition, each book in the series includes photographs, annotated bibliographies, timelines, and comprehensive indexes. For both the casual reader and the student researcher, the People in the News series offers insight into the lives of today's newsmakers—people who shape the way we live, work, and play in the modern age.

The Underdog Takes the Stage

Anyone who has listened to Eminem's lyrics knows that the man born as Marshall Mathers rose from an impoverished, troubled childhood. He has now become the best-selling rapper and one of the best-selling musicians of all time, making his story an unlikely one, in which he always casts himself as the underdog. Eminem struggled to get respect in the Detroit underground rap community and earned every bit he was given before catching his big break. Even now, after more than a decade as a major recording artist who has won more than a dozen Grammys, an Oscar, and countless other awards, Eminem still seems tentative to embrace his iconic place in the history of rap music.

The Story of the Underdog

Eminem was an underdog in several ways. As a white man in a predominantly black musical genre, Eminem's race was a component of his struggle to be respected in the rap industry. He was often booed when he took the stage—until he opened his mouth. Eminem had to prove himself on those stages, and he did, with his wicked word skills and a propensity to spin humorous freestyle raps in which he often made fun of himself.

His upbringing, too, contributed to his underdog persona. While typical rap narratives focus on the experience of being part of an oppressed race, Eminem rapped about the experience of being part of an oppressed underclass. For Eminem, this meant

Eminem's authenticity when rapping about his experiences with poverty, drugs, and violence gained him respect in a genre dominated by black artists.

that many of the things he rapped about—low paying jobs, burglaries, drugs, struggles to raise kids—were similar to the experience his black counterparts rapped about, but the distinction was important. It gave Eminem legitimacy with raps focused on his own survival in tough circumstances.

Eminem also saw himself as the underdog because of the abuse he took in his life, from playground and neighborhood bullies, uncaring teachers, an unbalanced mother, and a girlfriend whose temper was as volatile as his own. In his music, he often made fun of himself, criticizing himself as these people did or would, and ranting against opponents who would try and keep him down. This mixture of self-loathing and rebellion broadly appealed to teenagers of all kinds, black and white, urban and suburban, all of whom rooted for Eminem. Indeed, millions of fans connected with the image of the underdog—the man always struggling—that Eminem injected into his songs. That this persona often struggled through violence-tinged narratives, drug-laden jokes, and clouds of self-loathing ironically brought more fans to his side, especially suburban white teenagers, and increased his fame beyond what anyone, including himself, expected.

Once Eminem broke onto the national scene with the help of Dr. Dre, his success was unprecedented for a rap artist. Some said there was no explanation for his fame. Music critic Jon Caramanica reflects, "[Eminem's] pop megasuccess was serendipitous, explicable by no common measuring sticks."[1] Others regard it as carefully calculated. Almost everyone agrees Eminem is a uniquely talented word artist, but some, such as sociologist Edward G. Armstrong, maintain that Eminem's "discovery" was the result of Dr. Dre's search for a specifically white rap star he could market to white teenagers, an at that time yet untapped market for hip-hop music.

A Lot of Gas Left in the Tank

Though few would classify a multimillion-dollar rap celebrity as an underdog, Eminem still saw his life through the same lens that he always had, even after he made it big. While his financial concerns disappeared, the struggles of keeping up with the record executives' expectations and the demands of fans weighed equally heavily on him. And, troubled relationships continued to plague his life. When people began loudly claiming Eminem needed to be responsible for the violent and homophobic language in his music, Eminem again framed himself as the underdog in the fight. He brashly defended his right to free speech, to exercising his art, and angrily claimed he should not have to be anyone's role model.

Despite not wanting to be a role model, Eminem believes his story is widely appealing. Because he beat so many odds in his rise to fame—the trap of poverty, family dysfunction, marital conflict, and drug addiction—he believes people of all stripes can connect with his triumphs—and his record sales and popularity support this belief.

When Eminem emerged from his five-year hiatus from recording, he was stronger than ever and is now perhaps ready to accept a different role—one of role model. In his 2010 song, "Not Afraid," Eminem offers a hand to anyone who's been down a dark road. "I'm grateful for every fan letter I get and for every person who says I helped save them," he maintains. "I feel like I've got a lot of gas in the tank."[2]

Chapter 1

Instability and Hardship

Eminem was born Marshall Bruce Mathers III on October 17, 1972, in St. Joseph, Missouri, to parents Marshall Bruce Mathers Jr. (Bruce) and Debbie Nelson. From the very start, Marshall's life was filled with hardship, instability, and troubled relationships. Ultimately, Marshall's bottled feelings about his life's circumstances would find expression in rap music. Rapping gave Marshall an outlet for the anger he felt at all the trouble in his life and provided an art form through which the naturally shy boy could confidently express himself.

Young Love

Bruce Mathers and Debbie Nelson met when she was fourteen years old in her hometown of St. Joseph, Missouri. Debbie came from a troubled household, where she felt unloved by her mother and afraid of her abusive stepfather. She spent as much time as she could at friends' houses. When she met Bruce, a twenty-year-old drummer, she fell in love easily. He was kind to her and those around her, making her feel protected and wanted, a contrast to her home life. Bruce talked to Debbie about a future with a nice home filled with love and kids.

The couple decided they wanted to get married, but Debbie had to get her mother's permission to marry so young. She hounded her mother, threatening to run away or become pregnant when her mother would not sign the parental consent form Missouri required for underage marriages. Finally, her mother gave in, and Debbie and Bruce married on September 20, 1970, when Debbie was just fifteen years old. Early in their marriage Debbie and Bruce played together in a band, called Daddy Warbucks. The band toured Ramada Inns along the border of Montana and the Dakotas.

Two years into their marriage, Debbie gave birth to Marshall. Both Debbie and Bruce were very excited about the pregnancy; they had been hoping for over a year for a child. Debbie's labor was long and hard; she developed a condition known as toxicoma blood poisoning. After Marshall's birth, she was in a coma for three days. When she came to, she was introduced to her son who had been named by his father after himself. Though Bruce hadn't consulted Debbie on calling the baby Marshall Bruce Mathers III, she loved the name, since she loved his family.

By the time baby Marshall arrived, the relationship between Debbie and Bruce was turning sour. By Debbie's accounts, Bruce had begun to be abusive with her, frequently got drunk and had started to use drugs, and she suspected he was seeing other women. Whatever the reason, Bruce did not stay with the young family much longer. When Marshall was six months old, Bruce abandoned his family, eventually moving to California.

"We Moved Every Two or Three Months"

Debbie Nelson became a single mother at seventeen. She had no high school degree, no way to pay for rent, food, or diapers. She went to beauty school but struggled afterward to keep a job and pay for things on her own. She survived and supported Marshall with the help of welfare and family. When she was unable to provide herself and her son with a place to live, she moved in with family members.

As a result, Marshall bounced from home to home and city to city. When he was five, he and his mother moved to a run-down section of Detroit. Soon after, they moved back to Missouri, this time to Kansas City. By the time he was eleven, they were back in Detroit, only to be uprooted again soon after and go back to

Eminem's childhood was marked by poverty and frequent moves from home to home and city to city.

Missouri. "We were just staying wherever we could, with my grandmother, or whatever family would put us up," remembers Eminem. "It seemed like we moved every two or three months. I'd go to, like, six different schools in one year. We were on welfare, and my mom never worked."[3]

Moving around was difficult and confusing for Marshall. Even when he and his mother stayed in the same city, he remembers constantly moving between houses and apartments, leaving just before they were evicted because his mother could not pay the rent. While the experience of constantly moving was destabilizing, he found consistency in a few members of his extended family. His uncle Ronnie was just a few months older than him and became his best friend. Marshall's great-aunt Edna and granduncle Charles in Kansas City took care of him a lot. They brought him to school, let him stay over on weekends, took him shopping, and let him watch television. Marshall's fondest childhood memories were of being at their house.

Detroit

Detroit has historically been the capital of the automobile industry in America. When automobiles were invented and began to be manufactured, the influx of wealth to the city contributed to a gilded age in which Detroit became known as the "Paris of the West." In the twentieth century, the industrialization

Hitsville USA, the historic home of Motown Records, is a landmark of Detroit's rich musical history.

of auto factories drew large numbers of immigrants and African Americans who came to the city seeking the numerous blue-collar labor jobs that paid well.

The city's large African American population turned Detroit into one of America's strongest cities for music production and nightlife in the sixties and seventies. This most notably included Motown Records, which promoted artists such as Stevie Wonder and Diana Ross and the Supremes. Highways built in the second half of the twentieth century led to urban flight, in which huge numbers of people left the Detroit metro area for the suburbs. Eminem, Proof, and their Detroit rap group are proud to hail from inner-city Detroit rather than the suburbs. Detroit's area code is 313, which they often mention in their lyrics or wear on their clothes or as tattoos

Edna and Charles were his father's aunt and uncle. When Marshall was eight or nine, he remembers that his father would call Edna and Charles's house while he was there. Though Marshall could overhear the conversation, his father never asked to speak to him. Marshall always felt confused and hurt by this since he had never had any contact with his father that he could remember. This hurt turned to anger as young Marshall grew older. "It takes a real special kind of [expletive] to abandon a kid. To keep in touch with other family members—like his uncle—but not even get on the phone with a kid who did nothing wrong."[4]

In addition to moving often, Marshall was always acutely aware of his mother's struggles with money. Because they were on welfare, Marshall received free lunch at school, and his mother received food from the government to help them get by. Marshall often felt ashamed about both of these things and tried to hide them from his friends. There were times in his life when he only owned a few pairs of pants. He remembers his mother making him wear rolled up pajama bottoms to school as if they were shorts. "I'm not trying to give someone a sob story, like, 'Oh, I've been broke all my life' but people who know me know its true," he says. "There were times when friends had to buy me [expletive] shoes! I was poor white trash, no glitter, no glamour."[5]

A Bully Goes Too Far

Moving often meant that Marshall attended several different schools. He hated always being the "new kid." As a boy, Marshall was small and did not make friends easily. By the time he got close to new friends, he and his mother moved again. Constantly being the new kid was difficult and frustrating; these experiences made the naturally shy Marshall turn inward. He spent a lot of time alone.

Marshall was constantly picked on and bullied; he came to expect it every time he switched schools. Kids in each school would find things about Marshall to make fun of—his hair, his clothes, his size. He got beat up in hallways and bathrooms and pushed into lockers on a daily basis. When he was ten years old in the fourth grade, a particular sixth-grade boy, De'Angelo Bailey, made Marshall's life especially difficult. After weeks of trouble, Bailey beat up Marshall on the school playground. He smashed Marshall's head into a snow bank, leaving him unconscious on the playground. When Marshall woke up, he went home but quickly realized he was far from all right. His mother angrily accused the ten year old of being on drugs because he was acting strange. Then blood began to seep out of Marshall's ear; his mother immediately took him to the emergency room.

Marshall had suffered a cerebral hemorrhage at the hands of De'Angelo Bailey. The hemorrhage was severe—Marshall went into a coma shortly after being admitted to the hospital and did not regain consciousness for five days. Doctors were not convinced that Marshall would awake from this coma or that his mental capacity would be the same afterward. Marshall did wake up. The injury did not leave permanent physical damage, but the experience weighed heavily on Marshall.

Introduced to Rap

When Marshall was eleven, his uncle Ronnie turned him on to rap. The first rap Ronnie played for Marshall was "Reckless" by Ice-T, from the *Breakin'* soundtrack. From the moment Marshall heard the song, he wanted to get his hands on all the rap music he could find. Ronnie had two tape decks in his room. He used one to play the beat of the music and the other to record the raps he would recite over the music. Marshall took these tracks home and listened to them again and again. Listening to those tapes made him realize he wanted to rap himself.

Ronnie and Marshall were only a few months apart in age; they grew up together and were best friends. Ronnie was Marshall's mother's youngest brother; Marshall's grandmother had given birth to Ronnie late in life. Marshall and Ronnie hung out often during the years Marshall and his mom lived in Missouri. Shortly after Ronnie introduced Marshall to rap, Marshall and his mother moved back to Detroit. When Marshall visited Missouri again the next summer, Ronnie had left his interest in rap behind. He had gotten into heavy metal and wearing cowboy boots. Marshall, however, was hooked on rap.

The music of rapper Ice-T was introduced to Eminem when he was eleven years old by his uncle, whose own interest in rap music was an early influence.

Freestyle Battle Rap

In freestyle battle rapping, two emcees perform on the same stage using spontaneous raps to see who has better verses and skills. Battle rapping usually involves a lot of bragging and boasting, as well as insults, digs, and put-downs directed at the opposing MC. In addition to needing to execute good verses and spontaneously pull out raps that one-up and insult one's opponent, an important element of battle rap is also keeping one's composure when insulted. Talking with MTV, Eminem revealed his "secret" to being a successful battle rapper—preparation: "I would have written lines, I would have punchlines, that I would be prepared to say at anytime to kinda figure out on the spot what punchlines I would pick and choose for this person that was in my face but also be able to mix in freestyle with it. That would be the basic formula that I would follow, have my punchlines ready to go but also be able to say something spontaneous too."

A scene from Eminem's movie 8 Mile *depicts a freestyle rap battle.*

One of Eminem's other signature moves was to make fun of things about himself, such as his being white, before an opponent had the chance to insult him. Beating his opponent to the punch left them without anything bad to say about him that he had not already said about himself.

Quoted on MTV.com. "Eminem Gives Out His Secrets," June 15, 2010. www.mtv.co.uk/news/eminem/226091-eminem-gives-out-his-secrets.

For Marshall, rap was emotional, raw, and direct, full of gritty tales of life on the street. Listening to the music lifted Marshall out of his bullied, impoverished, miserable existence. He connected to the way rap artists told the truth about their lives with confidence and bravado; they could be angry, funny, or sad in their raps, as well as over-the-top and comically violent. Marshall also connected with the image of emcees (MCs—microphone controllers, i.e. rappers); to him they seemed like real people, dressing the way regular people did.

By the time Marshall was fourteen years old, he knew he wanted to be a rapper. He started to write his own raps and consumed all the hip hop he could get his hands on. "I spent a lot of time by myself, so hip-hop became my girl, my confidant, my best homie,"[6] he says.

Through rap, Marshall developed confidence and discovered he had a unique talent for rhyming and word play. Even though Marshall never liked to read books, he was always good at English. He began reading the dictionary just to have new words at his disposal. He ditched school to sneak into freestyle rap battles in the cafeteria of nearby Osborn High School. There he tested his skills, made new friends, and began to make a name for himself. DeShaun Holton, aka Proof, Marshall's best friend in high school, remembers, "It was like *White Men Can't Jump*. Everybody thought he'd be easy to beat [because he was a white kid] and they got smoked every time."[7]

Crossing 8 Mile

When Marshall was twelve, he and his mother moved from Kansas City to Warren, Michigan, to live with his grandmother. Debbie Nelson had just given birth to Marshall's half-brother, Nathan, and could no longer afford to live on her own in Missouri. Then, just before Marshall began the ninth grade—when he was fourteen— his mother was able to afford a house on the other side of 8 Mile Road, on Dresden Street, on the East Side of Detroit. 8 mile Road divides Warren, Michigan—a suburban area that is home to mostly white people—from the East Side of Detroit, a low-income area that is home to mostly black people. On Dresden

Road, on the East Side of Detroit, Marshall's family was one of only three white families in the neighborhood. Marshall, however, was still enrolled in his old school, Lincoln High School, in Warren. Rather than transfer schools and have to make friends all over again, he chose to make the two-mile walk to school and home everyday.

Though Marshall crossed 8 Mile to go to Lincoln High School in Warren, he spent a significant amount of time participating in rap battles in the school cafeteria of Osborn High School on the East Side of Detroit. Rap had become Marshall's way of life—Marshall sounded like a rapper and had adopted the style and dress of hip-hop culture. Since Marshall grew up in predominantly black neighborhoods as well as white ones, he felt at home in either and thought nothing of his devotion to a primarily black style of music. He often encountered problems, however, no matter which side of 8 Mile Road he was on.

As a kid I hated crossing 8 Mile and going into Warren, into hillbilly territory, and getting called a 'wigger' [a derogatory term for a white person who embodies aspects of black culture]. The fact that I loved hip-hop, just the fact that I rapped in school—some people thought it was cool and some people thought it was bull . . . but coming home [to East Detroit] crossing 8 Mile and getting jumped ... I was tested a lot.[8]

A Childhood Marked By Violence and Abuse

By now Marshall was used to being singled out for harassment, though as he got older Marshall started to fight back. His best friend, Proof, taught him how to stand up and fight. The two would bare-knuckle box in Marshall's front yard then would go inside to practice their rap lyrics. Despite his growing strength, Marshall still found himself the target of neighborhood violence. When he was fifteen, Marshall suffered a severe beating at the hands of a pack of men in a parking lot near his house. A passing car filled with guys flipped Marshall off; Marshall gestured back. They parked the car and came back after him. "One dude came up, hit me in the face and knocked me down. Then he pulled out a gun. I ran right out of my shoes, dog."[9] A truck driver who saw the beating chased the men off with his own gun, saving Marshall.

Violence was a large part of Marshall's life, both on the streets and in his family. "Guns and violence have been around me my whole life—in my family, in my social life,"[10] he notes. When he was just a kid, his uncles would take him to the gun range. They had AK-47s. He remembers handling his uncle's Colt .45 when he was just seven. His uncle would set up beer cans in the driveway for Marshall to shoot at. The same uncle was later convicted for killing a man in a parking lot with the same gun.

Marshall was also surrounded by abuse. Though he has never said he was abused, Ronnie was often beaten at the hands of a stepfather, and Debbie Nelson was constantly entangled in relationships with

DeShaun Holton, who went on to have a career as a rapper by the name of Proof, befriended Eminem when they were in their early teens. The friends worked together on both their fighting and rapping skills.

From M&M to Eminem

Eminem began using the stage name M&M in high school, when he was rapping in the Osborn High School cafeteria. M&M represented his initials—Marshall Mathers. Sometime before the release of his album *Infinite,* he changed his stage name from M&M to its phonetic equivalent: Eminem. He worried that if he ever made it big, he would run into legal issues sharing a stage name with a licensed candy product.

abusive men. It seemed that all the men in Marshall's life turned to guns or physical violence to deal with their problems or anger. Usually, however, Marshall chose to rap.

A Chaotic Home

Marshall attended Lincoln High School from 1986 to 1989. He spent each of those years in the ninth grade. After failing his freshman year for the third time, due mostly to his low attendance and lack of interest, he dropped out completely. As soon as he turned fifteen, his mother began threatening to kick him out if he did not get a job. Marshall eventually left school for minimum wage jobs and a chance to focus more on his music.

According to Marshall, he and his mother had a continually bad relationship. Though he did get steady jobs as a teenager, she would kick him out anyway, sometimes after she took most of his paycheck. Marshall remembers his mom taking lots of pills and smoking marijuana. She often seemed unbalanced, and Marshall remembers that she would wake up from naps and scream at whomever was in the house. Debbie Nelson denies these descriptions and that she ever kicked Marshall out. Nonetheless, Marshall's grandmother has confirmed that he often showed up on the doorstep of her trailer in Warren needing a place to sleep and has said publicly that Debbie was not a good mother.

The Eminem-Kim Saga Begins

Further complicating the relationship between Marshall and his mother was Kim Scott. Marshall and Kim met when he was fifteen years old. "I met her the day she got out of a youth home," he remembers. "She's thirteen, she's taller than me, and she didn't look that young. She easily coulda been mistaken for sixteen, seventeen. I said to my friend's sister, 'Yo, who was that? She's kinda hot.' And the saga began."[11]

Kim also came from a troubled family. She and her twin sister were frequently sent to live in the local youth home and often ran away. When Kim was thirteen years old, she moved in with Marshall and his mother because Marshall said she had no where else to go. She was one of several children Nelson fostered in her home throughout Marshall's childhood. When Kim moved in, the household became even more chaotic.

Kim constantly fought with both Nelson and Marshall; however, with Marshall the childish arguing and wrestling eventually made them inseparable, first as friends and then as a romantic couple. The two began dating and moved in together in 1989 when Marshall was seventeen—the year he dropped out of school.

The relationship was always volatile, off and on again. Proof, Marshall's best friend, had been around the two since they met. He remembers one fight in which Kim threw all of Marshall's clothes out on the lawn. "Em's like, 'I'm leaving her; I'm never going back.' Next day, he's back with her." Proof said of their relationship, "There's always gonna be conflict there."[12] Proof was right. Conflict was always a significant part of the relationship between Kim and Marshall; yet they always seemed inexplicably linked. The love Marshall shared with Kim, and the extreme anger she incited in him, became emotional and lyrical material for his raps.

Newlyweds Eminem and Kim Mathers, left, attend an album launch party in 2000. The couple began their volatile relationship as teenagers.

A Devastating Loss

In 1999, Marshall received devastating news. During a bout of depression, his uncle Ronnie committed suicide with a shotgun blast to the head. Marshall took the loss extremely personally. "I didn't talk for days. I couldn't even go to the funeral."[13] Ronnie was family, a close friend, and the person who introduced Marshall to rap. In his honor, Marshall got one of his first tattoos—"RIP Ronnie"—on his left upper arm.

Losing Ronnie was the latest tragedy in a childhood marked by instability, poverty, and violence. Rather than respond to these problems with more violence, however, Marshall found an outlet for his feelings in rap, into which he channeled his anger. With a talent for wordplay and rhythm, Marshall used his life as material. "My music is kinda like therapy to me," he once said. "Instead of bottling it up inside, I put it down on paper and spit it out on a mike."[14] Soon, Marshall would get the chance to share his intense feelings with the world.

Chapter 2

The Road to Success

Dropping out of school and moving out of his mother's house did not change Eminem's life much. He still had trouble finding a steady place to live, having enough money, and dealing with the volatile relationships that surrounded him. Rap was the only consistent thing in his life. In his late teens and early twenties he participated in rap battles all over Detroit, making a name for himself in the underground rap scene. The wider world of rap, however, was uninterested in Eminem until he created his angry, over-the-top, darkly comic alter-ego, Slim Shady.

A Crossroads

After dropping out of high school, Eminem had little option other than to work minimum-wage jobs. He took a low-paying dish-washing gig at Little Caesars Pizza with his best friend Proof. A few years later, he moved to Gilbert's Lodge, where he was a line cook and dishwasher. His pay there topped out at $5.50 an hour. Just as he did when he was a child, Eminem moved around a lot. Even working full-time, minimum wage did not give Eminem quite enough money to live on. At various points he lived with Kim Scott, friends, or at times even moved back in with his mother.

Eminem was confused about what to do with his life. The only thing he really wanted to do was be a rapper, but he also knew that making it was a long shot. He was not sure the hip-hop

Vanilla Ice was one of the first white rap artists to gain commercial success, but his popularity plummeted when it was discovered that he had made up details of his upbringing.

scene would embrace a white rapper—especially after Vanilla Ice. Vanilla Ice, one of the only white rappers to have made it big in the 1990s, quickly became an embarrassment when it was revealed that his life story, which supposedly influenced his lyrics, was made up to make him sound more street tough than he actually was. Eminem worried that hip-hop fans might always be suspicious of his legitimacy as a white rapper. "Vanilla Ice had made it damn near impossible for a white kid to get respect in rap music,"[15] he once said.

Nonetheless, Eminem spent all his free time rapping. After getting home from work close to midnight, he and his roommates would sit on the front porch until the early morning hours, drinking, freestyle rapping, and writing lyrics. When he was living in a house in East Detroit, Eminem gave up his bedroom so he and his friends had somewhere to put a mic and turntable.

The Bass Brothers

Once Eminem or his buddies recorded a song, they took the tape to a weekly radio show known as Open Mic. One Friday evening in 1992, Mark Bass heard Eminem's song and called into the radio studio. Mark and his brother Jeff made up Funky Bass Team (F.B.T.) Productions—a producing duo that was looking to take on new artists. After Mark convinced Jeff to give Eminem a shot, they signed him to their label and brought him into the studio to make a three-song demo.

Eminem, however, had little idea what to do with the demo tapes. He put them on consignment in local record shops, but few sold. The Bass brothers had connections in the hip-hop industry, but the record executives they approached with Eminem's songs were not interested. They said Eminem sounded too young. Nonetheless, the Bass brothers continued to work with Eminem, giving him time in the studio to experiment with his style and to write songs with the hope of recording a full-length album.

Becoming a Father

In 1995, Kim Scott became pregnant with Eminem's child. Hailie Jade Mathers was born on Christmas Day, 1995. Becoming a father brought life into quick focus for Eminem. From the moment Hailie was born, Eminem knew that he wanted to provide a good life for her and spare her the instability and dysfunction of his own childhood. With few other options, Eminem looked at rap as the only way out of poverty. His devotion to rap now became fueled by his desire to do right for Hailie. "Hailie being born was like an extra kick in the [butt]," he said. "Like, I don't do something now, I'm gonna be caught in the same sort of cycle of dysfunction that the rest of my family is in."[16]

Despite this desire, Eminem and Scott had a difficult time making ends meet. Earning just $5.50 an hour at Gilbert's Lodge made it difficult for Eminem to provide food, diapers, and a steady place to live for his family. Scott, Eminem, and Hailie moved constantly during Hailie's early life—from living with Eminem's mother, to living in the attic of Scott's mother's house, to renting a house that was often burglarized. Life was difficult; as he had in the past, Eminem channeled his feelings, frustrations, and anger into his music.

The Hip Hop Shop

Once Hailie was born, Eminem rarely got out to rap in public, though he spent a lot of time listening and writing lyrics. His friend Proof was always on him to keep his rhyme and lyric skills up. Proof organized a weekly battle at The Hip Hop Shop, a clothing store. The Hip Hop Shop had become the place to make a name in Detroit rap. If someone was good; the crowd let them know. If the rapper did not measure up, the crowd booed them out the door. Proof convinced Eminem to get on stage just once to see what kind of response he got.

Proof was strategic about introducing his white friend to the scene. He told Eminem to come the day a big battle was happening, but to come at the end when the shop was clearing out. This way Eminem would get feedback from a smaller group of people. Eminem showed up twenty minutes before the whole show was over. He rapped on stage and received amazingly positive reactions—people were screaming and jumping up and down. "I was the only white dude rapping in there and I was getting love, finally getting the respect I had dreamed of," he said. "Even though it was a small circle—it didn't matter. I finally had acceptance. Feeding off that energy made me come back the next week, and the next week, and the next week."[17]

Eminem began organizing his work schedule at Gilbert's Lodge around his performances. Week after week, his audiences grew larger and larger, and Eminem's confidence grew. Soon, Eminem became the person to beat in battles around the city, and even got paid for his performances.

Rock Bottom

In 1995, Eminem wrote material for an album that would be recorded by F.B.T Productions in their new studio, the Bassment. The album, *Infinite*, was recorded shortly after Hailie's birth and released in 1996 by Web Entertainment, an independent label created by the Bass brothers. The album's lyrics were written mostly while Kim Scott was pregnant with Eminem's daughter. They reflect Eminem's dreams of making it big and his anxiety

An Excuse to Let Go

The alter-ego that Eminem created for himself became a vehicle whereby he released the anger he had for his girlfriend, his living situation, his terrible childhood. Using the persona helped him to hold nothing back. In this way, Slim Shady became more than an alter-ego; Eminem found himself in Slim Shady. He describes this transformation in the following way: "The more I started writing and the more I slipped into this Slim Shady character, the more it just started becoming me. My

Eminem performs on stage as his alter-ego, Slim Shady.

true feelings were coming out, and I just needed an outlet to dump them in. I needed some type of persona. I needed an excuse to let go of all this rage, this dark humor, the pain, and the unhappiness."

Eminem. *Angry Blonde*. New York: Regan Books, 2000, p. 3.

Members of D12, a rap group created by Eminem and Proof, appear at the 2004 MTV Music Awards.

over raising and providing for his child. The album got some attention, but was largely criticized as having an unoriginal voice, sounding too much like other popular rappers of the time.

The negative response to the album was the last straw for an increasingly frustrated Eminem. Shortly before Christmas 1996, Eminem was fired from his job. He tried to find work when he could, briefly returning to Little Caesars. Life became so hard—trying to make ends meet while raising Hailie—that he stopped writing and rapping. He turned to drugs as times became more difficult. He and Scott fought constantly, regularly breaking and making up. Eventually she and Hailie moved back in with her family, and Eminem moved in with his mother. Since Scott's family had never liked Eminem, the living situation made it difficult for him to even see Hailie.

One night, he felt so desperate and angry he took too many drugs and spent the night vomiting. It was one of Eminem's lowest points, an incident that many called a suicide attempt. Eminem does not believe he was trying to end his life, but agrees it was the worst point in a difficult time. He turned the circumstances that led up to the night into music, and these became the lyrics for his song "Rock Bottom."

D12 and the Creation of Slim Shady

Eminem continued to perform in battles, often collaborating with his best friend Proof. Proof had the idea to create a band of Detroit MCs in a loose collective, like the East Coast's Wu-Tang Clan. Together Eminem and Proof invited six rappers to be a part of the group. Several of them were high school friends Eminem had battled with at Osborn High School. Eminem and Proof chose skilled rappers, but ones who were not already on the inside of Detroit's hip-hop scene. Once chosen, the six rappers worked together to create songs, but also competed for space on tracks. Working like this made the group close friends. They made a pact: "Whoever makes it out first will come back for the rest."[18]

Proof had initially hoped to have twelve emcees so that he could call the group the Dirty Dozen (D12). On the way home from a rap convention in New York, Proof floated a new idea. Each of the six members would create a dark alter-ego. The alter-ego would allow the group to number twelve and give each rapper the opportunity to experiment with hardcore rap styles. "The whole thing in D12 was to have a personality where you would just say anything," Proof explained. "Your persona was almost like a mask to hide behind."[19]

Eminem was the last member of D12 to create his alter ego. In the summer of 1997, he was still having a rough time. He worked a lot (when he had a job), drank a lot, fought with Scott, and struggled to raise Hailie. One morning, he came up with the character Slim Shady in the place where he often did thinking: the bathroom. "The name just hit me," he explains. "When I thought of the name Slim Shady, I started thinking of a million things to rhyme with it. And that was just the turning point. I realized that this alter-ego was going to become more than just shock rap. It wasn't that I just wanted to shock people. There was part of me coming out too. Like me being pissed off at the world."[20]

The 1997 Rap Olympics

Slim Shady did the trick: once Eminem came up with the Slim Shady concept, he wrote the *Slim Shady* EP in two weeks. *The Slim Shady* EP was recorded and released by the Bass brothers on their independent label, Web Entertainment. The EP's five main songs mark a complete departure from Eminem's style on

Eminem recorded songs for his Slim Shady EP in a nondescript building in Ferndale, Michigan, in 1997.

Infinite—these raps feature constant over-the-top violence, references to drug use and sexual acts, and explore Eminem's difficult family and financial situations. They also use self-deprecating humor to thwart potential critics. Compared with *Infinite*, this album garnered significant underground attention—attention that followed Eminem to the 1997 Rap Olympics.

In October 1997 Eminem flew to Los Angeles to compete in the Rap Olympics. He literally didn't have a dime to his name before the trip—his plane ticket was given to him by Wendy Day. Day was the chief executive officer of the Rap Coalition, a not-for-profit artists' advocacy group. Though Eminem was excited for the chance to compete, he lost his battle in the very last round. He was furious, because he had been counting on the first place winnings. "I took second place and I was very unused to that. Everyone said I looked like I was ready to cry. And I was so mad. Steaming, dog. I had nowhere to live back home. The winner of the Rap Olympics got, like, five hundred dollars. I could have used that, man. Second place got nothing."[21] When Eminem walked away from the Rap Olympics venue, Dean Geistlinger from Interscope Records asked if he could have a demo. Eminem was in such a terrible mood, he simply threw the *Slim Shady* EP at him and kept going.

"I Had to Meet Him Right Away"

Dean Geistlinger turned out to be an assistant to Jimmy Iovine, the chairman of Interscope Records. Once Iovine got the tape, he played it for rapper Dr. Dre. Dr. Dre remembered Eminem's voice from a radio show that Eminem and other Rap Olympics artists participated in right after the event. As soon as Eminem's voice came through Iovine's speakers, Dr. Dre wanted to sign him. This was very unusual: Dr. Dre had never discovered anyone through a demo tape. "Usually somebody knew somebody or someone was brought up to the studio," said Dr. Dre. But this was different; it grabbed him. "When I heard it I didn't even know he was white. The content turned me on more than anything, and the way he was flipping it. Dark comedy is what I call it. It was incredible. I had to meet him right away."[22]

Dr. Dre, left, discovered Eminem after listening to a demo tape of the Slim Shady EP. He went on to produce Eminem's first mainstream release, 1999's Slim Shady.

Dr. Dre

Dr. Dre (born Andre Young) initially became famous in the mid-1980s as a part of N.W.A., a West Coast rap group from Compton, California. N.W.A. was known for violent descriptions of street life, making it one of the founders of gangsta rap. Dre eventually went solo. His first album, *The Chronic*, became the best-selling album of 1992 and turned Dr. Dre into rap royalty. After his initial success, Dre focused on producing music for other artists under his label, Aftermath Entertainment.

Dre has a passion for cultivating new rap artists. He used his status to launch other artists into their own successful careers, starting with Snoop Dog. Dr. Dre is also frequently the producer on individual songs for a wide variety of artists, which have included Mary J. Blige, Eve, Gwen Stefani, Jay-Z, Timbaland, and Queen Latfah.

Within a week, Eminem went back to LA to meet Dr. Dre in the studio. Dr. Dre signed Eminem to produce his first mainstream, large-release album. The first day they worked together, the pair recorded four songs in six hours, the first of which was the infamous "My Name Is." Those who witnessed the recording remember it vividly. "Em came in real quiet, humble," remembers Richard "Segal" Huredia, the engineer on the "My Name Is" track. "Once he got on the mike, though, his energy came out, with him doing all these different voices—we'd never heard [anything] like that before. At one point, we were all just vibing to the beat, and he turns around and goes, 'Hi, my name is . . . ' We were like, 'That's kinda catchy.' "[23] Eminem impressed everyone in the studio. He was a perfectionist, who came ready with ideas and imagination to spin into rap songs.

For Eminem this break came at just the right time. Back in Detroit, he was out of places to live. The night before the Rap Olympics, he had been evicted from his house. In fact, the night before he caught his flight to Los Angeles, Eminem had to break into a house and sleep on the floor with no heat or lights. Eminem remembers, "When Dre called, he saved my life."[24]

Dr. Dre's name lent Eminem credibility in the hip-hop community. Just as in high school, initial listeners questioned whether a white man could rap. "It's like seeing a black guy doing country & western," said Dr. Dre once. "I got a couple of questions from people around me. You know, 'He's got blue eyes, he's a white kid.' But I don't [care] if you're purple: If you can kick it, I'm working with you."[25] Dr. Dre was confident in Eminem's talent; he took it upon himself to introduce him to the world and make him a star.

The Real Slim Shady

Based on his earlier *Slim Shady* EP he had recorded with F.B.T., the *Slim Shady LP* album was released on February 23, 1999. The album debuted to commercial and critical success. It was ranked second on the *Billboard* charts the week it was released and sold 283,000 copies in its first week. The lead single of the album, "My Name Is" was an instant hit. The video played constantly on MTV and radio stations. "My Name Is" introduced the world to Slim Shady, a comically dark, grotesque, willing to do and say anything character. It brought both rappers and pop music listeners to Eminem as fans. The album caught on so fast, Eminem became an instant celebrity. He appeared on the cover of *Rolling Stone* magazine barely two months after the album broke.

From the moment the album was released, however, there were complaints about its content. Eminem's lyrics contained substantial use of profanity, excessive descriptions of drug use and sexual acts, and a good bit of violence. In one of the most discussed songs, "'97 Bonnie and Clyde," Eminem raps about taking his toddler daughter to a beach to dispose of his wife's body, who he has fictionally murdered and stashed in the trunk. The album cover, in fact, shows a picture of him and his daughter standing at a pier, with a car in the background that has a woman's legs sticking out of the trunk. Eminem said this was not intended to

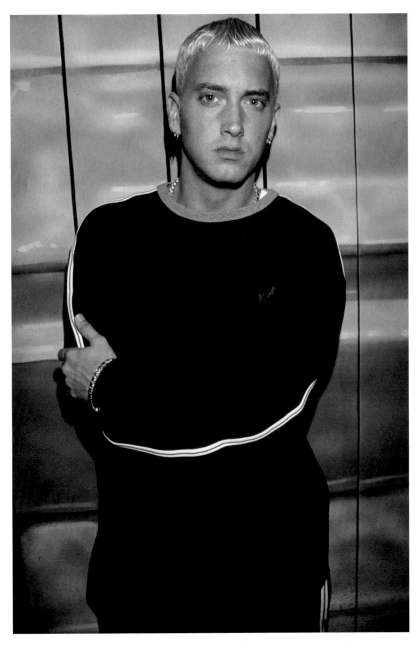

Eminem poses before the MTV Video Music Awards where he won Best New Artist for Slim Shady LP, which contained the hit song "My Name Is" and made the rapper an instant celebrity.

be taken literally. His songs were often dark, ironic and comical, not serious. As he put it, "I'm bringing cutting edge humor to hip-hop."[26]

The year ended with a major achievement for Eminem. *The Slim Shady LP* was honored at the Grammys, winning Best Rap Album. With the creation of his alter-ego Slim Shady and the following *Slim Shady* record, Eminem had made it—and everyone was waiting to see what he would say or do next.

Chapter 3

A Controversial Artist

After the success of the *Slim Shady LP*, Eminem did not let up. He embarked on an ambitious tour and continued to churn out rap hits that were as popular as they were offensive. Indeed, although Eminem created millions of fans in his rise to fame, he also created many enemies. Parents, teachers, and even government officials were offended by Eminem's explicit lyrics. Since he became popular in an era when bubble-gum boy bands and Britney Spears ruled the airwaves, his rage and violent talk toward women and gays made him stand out even further as a bad influence. Together, these issues have made Eminem one of the most controversial artists of the last decade.

The Marshall Mathers LP

On May 23, 2000, a little over a year after Eminem broke onto the national scene, his second album, *The Marshall Mathers LP*, was released. Much of the material that Eminem wrote for this album reflects his experience dealing with fast fame. Alter-ego Slim Shady is very present on this album—the album is as filled with violent tirades, especially toward women and gays, as his first CD had been; however, as is indicated by the fact that the album bears his real name, the overall tone is more personal. The most popular song of the album, "Stan," is one of Eminem's signature story songs. It depicts a fictional fan who becomes increasingly obsessed with Eminem. The album also features lyrics about

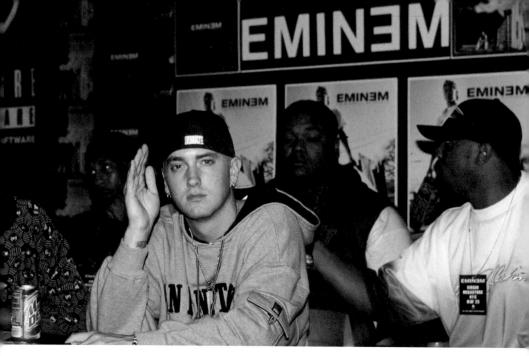

Eminem makes a record-store appearance to sign copies of The Marshall Mathers LP *in New York City soon after its release in May 2000.*

Kim Scott, as well as celebrities whom Eminem dislikes. While the lyrics are more serious and personal, they are also violent and laced with homophobic language.

The album garnered lots of attention. In its first week it sold more than 1.7 million copies, giving the album the record for best first week sales. In addition, *Marshall Mathers* became the fastest-selling rap album of all time, the fastest-selling album by a solo artist, and the second-fastest-selling album ever. This was especially significant because in 2000 pop artists ruled the music landscape, with the boy band 'N Sync and Britney Spears topping the charts.

Eminem's music, however, appealed to a broader audience. In addition to having songs that appealed to rap and pop fans, *Marshall Mathers* got airtime on rock radio stations, too. Radio stations across the country reported that requests for Eminem's music had them playing more songs from this album than any other. Indeed, *Marshall Mathers* spent eight weeks at number one on the *Billboard* charts, making the album the runaway hit of the summer of 2000.

Eminem, Producer

From the moment Eminem began working with Dr. Dre, he wanted to learn the ropes of production. Although he often planned out beats to back up his rap lyrics, he did not have the know-how or equipment to produce his own. With Dre, Eminem learned it all and wanted to create his own production label so he could produce his own beats and produce and release albums for others—most importantly, D12. He wanted to fulfill the pact that D12 members had made that whoever made it big would help out the others in the group.

Eminem promotes the release of D12's album Devil's Night *in New York City in 2001.*

To this end, after the release of *Slim Shady*, Eminem and his manager, Paul Rosenburg, created Shady Records, a label of Interscope Records. It was considered a boutique—or small scale—production company that benefited from the backing and release outlets of its parent production company. Eminem's first order of business was to sign a contract with D12 to produce and release their first album, *Devil's Night,* which came out in June 2001. It had taken several years, but Eminem had fulfilled the pact.

Critics for the most part celebrated Eminem's second album. "He is a master rhymer, convincing actor, stinging critic of critics, and vicious prankster," wrote music critic Neil Strauss in the *New York Times.* "He is blessed with the ability to make any two words with a letter in common rhyme."[27] The album earned Eminem his second consecutive Grammy for Best Rap Album and it was nominated for the first time in the category of Best Album of the Year.

"The Real Danger" of Eminem

Not everyone was a fan, however. In particular, the album's homophobic lyrics evoked much criticism. Many of Eminem's songs mention violence toward gays and gay rape, and in nearly every song Eminem uses the term *faggot*, a derogatory term for a gay person. In the song "Criminal," for example, Eminem raps that he hates "fags," and promises to stab gays and lesbians in the head with his words. On another track, "Kill You" Eminem threatens a gay person at knifepoint.

In Eminem's music, the Gay and Lesbian Alliance Against Defamation (GLAAD), found plenty of reason to be offended. They organized one of the largest protests of his music. GLAAD called *Marshall Mathers* "the most blatantly offensive" album to have been released in years. "While hate crimes against gay people are on the rise, these epithets create even more bias and intolerance toward an entire community," warned GLAAD. "The real danger comes from the artist's fan base of easily influenced adolescents, who emulate Eminem's dress, mannerisms, words, and beliefs."[28]

For this reason, GLAAD was offended in 2000 when MTV nominated Eminem for several MTV Music Awards and booked him to perform at the award show. GLAAD believed that by honoring Eminem, MTV promoted homophobia (fear and hatred of gay and lesbian people). They tried to have Eminem banned from the show. Although they were unsuccessful, MTV agreed to scale back their promotion of Eminem and aired a special that discussed the problem of gay intolerance in society.

Eminem has continually blown off concerns about his use of the word *faggot*, claiming he uses the word to refer to jerks. "For me the word 'faggot' has nothing to do with sexual preference," he once said. In typical Eminem fashion, criticism of his use of the word led him to push back harder. "When people got all up

Demonstrators offended by Eminem's lyrics rally outside of the 2001 Grammy Awards. Critics accused the rapper of promoting homophobia and advocating hate through his music.

in arms about it, I started to use it more just to piss them off even worse."[29] Eminem thought that controversy over his use of the word was one of the ways critics misunderstood the point of his songs. In his mind, a lot of what he raps is a joke, delivered in character, and not to be taken seriously. As he once told a *Rolling Stone* reporter, "If people would just listen to the lyrics, I say [in the song 'Criminal'], 'Half the [stuff] I say/I just make it up to make you mad.'"[30]

The Most Violent Rap Artist

Gay rights groups were not the only ones offended by Eminem. The album was also criticized for being misogynistic, or hateful of women. This charge was leveled by many, including Lynne Cheney, former chairman of the National Endowment for the

Humanities and wife of then vice presidential candidate Dick Cheney. Cheney was outraged that someone who spewed hateful lyrics about women would be publicly honored and held up as a role model. She even complained about Eminem in testimony before the Senate Commerce Committee hearing on violence in the media. "This is dreadful. This is shameful," she said of the lyrics of "Kill You," a song in which Eminem describes different ways to kill a woman. "Can you imagine that the entire industry honors this man whose work is so hateful?"[31] Cheney worried that honoring someone like Eminem sent a bad message to children.

Sociologist Edward G. Armstrong has studied the prevalence of violence in rap and concluded that Eminem's songs contain the most violence directed specifically toward women in all of music. Armstrong listened to numerous rap albums and rated each for the number and type of incidences of violence in each song. In a study published in 2004, Armstrong found that Eminem's music contained significantly more misogynistic content than average gangsta rap. The average gangsta rap album included descriptions of violence toward women in 22 percent of songs. On *Marshall Mathers*, however, eleven out of the fourteen songs—or 79 percent—contained descriptions of violence toward women. While *Marshall Mathers* was Eminem's most violent album, Armstrong found that all four of Eminem's albums averaged 63 percent violent content, making his music consistently more violent and misogynistic than average gangsta rap.

Armstrong also noted that Eminem was not simply violent; his music featured the murder and rape of women in ways new and different in rap music. On *Marshall Mathers*, for example, Eminem describes choking a woman, stabbing a woman, and killing her using a chainsaw and machete. He describes the drowning, head splitting, throat slitting, and shooting of women. A number of these references are preceded by rape. Gangsta rap as a genre generally includes references to murder and rape, but Eminem is by far the rapper who raps about this the most. Armstrong found that typical gangsta rap discusses violent murder and rape of women in about 38 percent of songs; Eminem's music, however, includes these topics in 72 percent of songs.

Not a Gun, a Microphone

Eminem defends his lyrics as a form of art, valid because they are an expression of his emotions in a specific recorded moment. "I haven't had the greatest experience with women," he told one interviewer. "You can get mad and record something at that moment and that's how you feel at the moment, and do you feel that way every single day when you wake up? No. . . . Music is about emotion, and capturing emotion right then and there while it's happening."[32]

In fact, Eminem has said that rapping about violence is his way of actually avoiding it. Rapping is his way of avoiding acting on his angry, violent impulses. Eminem said the song "'97 Bonnie and Clyde" was written after he and Kim had had a huge fight and broken up, and it reflected his frustration over their relationship. "The fact that a man picks up a microphone, that's it, you see?" he once told a reporter. "That's what makes him a rapper. It's not a gun. It's a microphone."[33]

Eminem as Role Model

Between his misogyny and his homophobia, people worried that Eminem was a negative influence on his teenage fans. Concerns that Eminem was contributing to a culture of hate were pervasive. As Joyce Hunter, a research scientist at Columbia University put it, "People say they can sing these lyrics and it doesn't mean anything. It means something."[34]

In response to these concerns, Eminem is quick to ask for evidence of any kid's acting out such violence to mimic something in his songs. He credits his audience as being smart enough to know that the characters he raps about are not role models—they are down and out, angry fools whose lives no one would want. Unlike a lot of rap stars, Eminem and his alter-egos have never touted street life as glamorous; Eminem bemoans street life—the poverty, violence, and familial dysfunction—in his music more than anything else.

Furthermore, Eminem says his music is not meant for children and teenagers. A parental warning label is slapped on the outside

Eminem performs for eager fans in Montreal, Canada, in April 2000. The rapper dismisses accusations that his songs have a negative influence on his audience, and he has stated that his music is not meant for children and teens.

Brand Eminem

In addition to launching Shady Records, his own recording label, Eminem has become associated with a clothing line (Shady Ltd.), a gaming company (Shady Games), movie properties, and most significantly, as of October 2004, a radio station. Sirius, the satellite radio company, debuted Shade 45, an uncensored, commercial-free hip-hop channel directed by the vision of Eminem.

Eminem is the executive producer of Shade 45, along with Shady Records, Interscope Records, and Sirius. Eminem hosts shows from time to time, recorded a special freestyle song for the channel, and directs some of the content, making the channel more new-music intensive than any of the other hip-hop channels Sirius carries. Sirius calls this initiative the most direct way a musician can reach fans—a way to connect twenty-four hours a day, even when a new album has not yet been put out by an artist.

of each of his albums to make clear that the music is inappropriate for children, and Eminem believes it is a parent's responsibility to decide and control what their kids listen to. "This is adult music, and yeah, it has that appeal where kids are going to like it, but that's where parents should step in and be a parent. Watch what your kids are listening to, because I do the same thing with my kids."[35] Eminem contends that he cannot be held responsible for parents' not exercising control over their kids.

"What Is the Big Deal About Eminem?"

Discussions of Eminem's music and the controversy surrounding his lyrics bled into the 2001 Grammy season. Eminem received three nominations, including Best Album of the Year for *Marshall Mathers*. As soon as the nominations were released, however, the National Academy of Recording Arts and Sciences (NARAS), the organization that organizes the Grammys, was swamped with criticism. Gay rights groups, women's rights groups, concerned parents, as well as fans responded in such overwhelming numbers that the organization's computer servers shut down. Phone lines were tied up, and mail flooded in. While some applauded the nominations, many wanted Eminem's nominations to be pulled entirely. Michael Greene, the head of NARAS, defended the nomination committee's decision, saying they could honor Eminem's recording without necessarily condoning its message. As Greene put it, "There's no question about the repugnancy of many of his songs. They're nauseating in terms of how we as a culture like to view human progress. But it's a remarkable recording and the dialogue that it's already started is a good one."[36]

Eminem was also defended by a large number of other artists, who supported his right to free speech. These included Stevie Wonder, LL Cool J, and Madonna, who wrote in the Los

Eminem and Elton John, left, acknowledge the audience after performing together at the Grammy Awards in 2001.

Angeles Times, "What is the big deal about Eminem? Since when is offensive language a reason for being unpopular? I find the language of [President] George W. [Bush] much more offensive. . . . [Eminem's] reflecting on what's going on in society right now. This is what art's supposed to do."[37] Several artists pointed out that being offensive was hardly a new thread in popular music and that expressing violence toward any group of people was not unique to rap.

Letting actions speak louder than words, Eminem countered criticisms by performing at the Grammys with Elton John, perhaps the most well known gay man in the world. Eminem sang one of his most popular songs with John, then held hands and hugged him. Many gays were flabbergasted that such a prominent gay artist and activist would choose to cooperate with Eminem, but John said he thought Eminem was one of the most talented artists alive. "I've always admired Eminem's thinking," said John. "That's the reason I wanted to appear with him when I was asked, despite all the nonsense talked about his being homophobic and crap like that. . . . Eminem has the balls to say what he feels and to make offensive things funny."[38]

Controversy on the Road

Criticism and controversy only seemed to boost Eminem's stature. Eminem was the newest, biggest thing in rap—and his appeal was crossing boundaries, bringing scores of white teenagers to rap. Less than a month after the release of *Marshall Mathers*, Eminem went on Dr. Dre's Up in Smoke tour. The lineup included legendary rappers Snoop Dogg, Ice Cube, and a number of other emcees. In large part because of Eminem's presence, Up in Smoke became the most successful rap tour in history.

Eminem was a force on stage. He performed in denim overalls and no shirt, wearing a hockey mask, and toting a chainsaw. He sometimes brought an unclothed inflatable doll on stage to kick around, calling it the names of celebrities or people in his personal life (such as Kim Scott), whomever he was most angry at. Eminem embraced the theatricality that large-scale performances allowed. Of course, not everyone was thrilled by his over-the-top

Eminem wears a mask and wields a chain saw while performing in 2001. The rapper's inclusion of violent and sexual images in his stage shows brought him much criticism and controversy.

antics. City Officials in Detroit, for example, attempted to prevent Eminem from carrying the naked inflatable doll on stage. They also threatened to arrest concert organizers if they showed a video that featured partial nudity and depicted a robbery.

Eminem's onstage antics continued after the Up in Smoke tour ended. For example, during one show on Limp Bizkit's Anger Management tour, Eminem tried to get the crowd to chant, "Take them drugs!" In another, he swallowed a number of white pills while performing. This stunt got Eminem investigated by the London police, who accused him of taking Ecstasy and encouraging drug use.

"Not a Single Emotion Is Faked"

Despite the demands of touring, Eminem managed to write and record another album during this time. *The Eminem Show* was released on May 23, 2002, exactly two years after *Marshall Mathers*. The album immediately topped the *Billboard* charts and sold 1.3 million copies in its first week. *The Eminem Show* continued to feature violent and homophobic lyrics. This album also chronicled Eminem's personal troubles, including strife with Kim Scott and his mother, as well as bouts of drug use.

Nonetheless, the album received many positive reviews. "*Eminem Show* is a rich autobiography, shocking because not a single word is made up and not a single emotion is faked," said music critic Robert Wilonsky. "Not in decades has a chart-topper so evoked and provoked; at long last, here's a pop star who makes you feel something."[39] Reflecting these reviews, *The Eminem Show* earned Eminem his third consecutive Grammy for Best Rap Album and was also nominated for Best Album of the Year.

As Exciting as Treading Water

Eminem's next studio album, *Encore,* was released on November 12, 2004. *Encore* enjoyed strong sales from the beginning; in its first three days it sold 710,000 copies. The album was received with generally positive reviews. However, fans and music critics alike noted that the quality of the lyrics and music was not up

8 Mile

In 2002, Eminem starred in *8 Mile*, a movie largely based on his life. Producer Brian Grazer thought Eminem's dramatic life story made him the perfect film subject. Eminem played Jimmy "B-Rabbit" Smith Jr., a poor, white rapper from a rough part of Detroit.

Eminem starred in the 2002 movie 8 Mile, which was based on his life and rise to fame.

Though the movie opened in a limited number of theaters and was rated R, it was the leading movie the November weekend it opened. *8 Mile* drew established Eminem fans and created new ones, giving Eminem his largest audience yet. Critics gave the movie glowing reviews. "This may be one of the few inspirational movies that could actually inspire someone, somewhere, sometime,"[1] wrote Richard Schickel of *Time* magazine. "Eminem is on fire,"[2] agreed Peter Travers in *Rolling Stone*.

In addition to the film's success, the soundtrack to *8 Mile* sold 250,000 copies its first week and became one of the top five best-selling albums of 2002, even though it was released late in the year. "Lose Yourself," the movie's signature track, which Eminem wrote while filming, topped charts in the United States and Europe and even won Eminem an Oscar for Best Original Song in a movie.

1. Richard Schickel. "Eminem *8 Mile High*." Time, November 11, 2002, p. 2.

2. Peter Travers. "Eminem Gets It Right." *Rolling Stone,* November 28, 2002, p. 97.

Eminem performs at the 2004 MTV Europe Music Awards days after the release of Encore, *which contained "Mosh," a song with a political theme.*

to the level of Eminem's earlier successes. "['The Eminem Show' and '8 Mile'] are big footsteps to follow, and "Encore" lags well behind," noted Neva Chonin in the *San Francisco Chronicle*. "The album is all but static, caught between Eminem's old brat-king persona and his evolving role as a hip-hop artist of conscience. It's the aural [sound] equivalent of treading water, and just about as exciting."[40]

While many agreed that much of the album was the same old thing, there were standout songs. For example, on this album, Eminem got political for the first time. The song "Mosh" criticized then-president George W. Bush for his handling of the Iraq War. The video was strategically released just a few days before the 2004 presidential election, in which Bush sought a second term. The video featured an army of protesters crashing in on a voter registration site to cast their votes against Bush. (After Bush was reelected, the ending was changed to show the army bursting in on Bush as he is about to give the state of the union speech).

Eminem said of the song, "I've never been one to be all that political . . . but my personal opinion—and I'm just one person who happens to speak to a lot of people—is that we live in the best country there is, and this guy is [messing] it up. There's people over there [in Iraq] dying and we can't get a straight answer why."[41] Eminem's point of view excited fans, critics, and columnists, some of whom praised Eminem for using his formidable rhyming skills and popularity in a productive way. As Sasha Frere-Jones of the magazine *The New Yorker*, put it, "At last: Eminem was behaving like the badass he'd always claimed to be."[42]

Keeping Up with Fame

Although "Mosh" was a widely celebrated song, it stood almost alone on the album for its style and depth. Even Eminem has said he was disappointed with the album. Like each of Eminem's previous albums, *Encore* was nominated for Best Rap Album; however, for the first time, the nomination did not win him the award.

Eminem had worked feverishly for six years. He had toured constantly, recorded four solo albums, created his own production company, cultivated new artists, and starred in a movie. He had become the biggest rapper in the world, as well as one of music's most popular artists. But the stressful nature of fame appeared to have caught up with him by the summer of 2005, when problems that had been brewing since he first became famous came to a head.

Chapter 4

Downward Spiral

Eminem's personal struggles endured even as he became a successful rap star. His troubled relationships with his mother and Kim Scott continued to worsen. Eminem's temper and use and abuse of drugs grew worse. These problems ultimately sidelined Eminem from the two things he loved most—his music and his daughter.

More Money, More Problems

Making it as a successful rap artist earned Eminem more money than he had ever seen in his life. Once royalty checks began to come in from the *Slim Shady* album, he, Kim Scott, and Hailie moved out of Scott's mother's house to a large house in Sterling Heights, a middle-class suburb of Detroit. The house had a pool, several bedrooms, and a large piece of land. Then, on June 14, 1999, Eminem and Kim married in a private ceremony in St. Joseph, Missouri, surrounded by Eminem's mother's relatives. Of their marriage, Eminem said, "Right now, I feel like I'm on top of the world. I did right for my daughter."[43]

But Eminem's newfound fame and wealth had other consequences, too. Long-lost relatives and acquaintances began to come out of the woodwork, contacting Eminem or showing up in the media, peddling stories about him. His father, who lives in San Diego, California, attempted to contact Eminem for the first time since Eminem was an infant. He even appeared on the TV news program *Inside Edition*, bemoaning his estrangement from his son and showing off photos of Eminem as a baby.

Eminem had little empathy for his father's newfound interest in him. Rather than speak directly to his father, Eminem responded through lyrics, rapping that he wished his deadbeat father was dead. Eminem could not forgive his father for abandoning him as a child. "If my kids were moved to the edge of the Earth, I'd find them," he said. "No doubt in my mind. No money, no nothin', if I had nothing, I'd find my kids. So there's no excuse. There's no excuse."[44]

Sued by His Mother

Eminem's mother also tried to benefit from her son's success. On September 17, 1999, Debbie Nelson filed suit against Eminem for $10 million, claiming that his lyrics and comments about her caused her emotional distress. Eminem was furious and maintained that everything he had ever said about his mother was true. He retaliated by making more negative comments about

Eminem's mother, Debbie Nelson, filed a lawsuit against her son in 1999, claiming that the negative portrayal of her in his music had caused her emotional distress.

his mother on *Marshall Mathers*. As he told one reporter, "If my mother is . . . cruel enough, knowing she didn't help me get where I'm at, try to take food out of my mouth and out of my daughter's mouth, try to take me for everything I have, then I'm not holding back on this album."[45]

The lawsuits did not end there. The following year, Nelson filed another lawsuit against her son, asking for another million dollars for emotional damages she suffered during the proceedings of the first lawsuit. The trials from these two suits dragged on for years. Ultimately the court awarded Nelson only twenty-five thousand dollars, and after all legal fees were paid, she took home only about sixteen hundred dollars. The more lasting result of the suits was a permanently fractured relationship between mother and son. For years afterward, Eminem still had little contact with his mother, despite the fact that he often cared for his younger half brother, Nathan. In a 2010 interview, Eminem commented, "It'd be very hard to repair that relationship"[46] because he did not even know where his mother was living.

Angry Blonde

Eminem himself found it difficult to cope with his newfound fame. Despite his stage persona, Eminem was still the shy, reserved person he had been as a child: quiet around new people but quick to anger when he felt threatened or violated. As a result, he was easily frustrated by the hordes of people who followed him in public. Eminem sometimes greeted his fans humbly and signed autographs with appreciation, but mostly he became enraged if fans impinged on his private life.

In particular, he hated when fans came to his house. Because a city ordinance would not allow him to build a fence around his land, his home and family were harassed by overeager fans, some of whom went swimming in his pool, stole his mailbox as a souvenir, or rang his doorbell and took photos when Eminem answered. Eminem did not handle the invasiveness well; he bought guns. He carried them even in the house and boasted that any person who came to his house uninvited would get the barrel of a gun in his/her mouth.

Eminem appears in a courtroom in Warren, Michigan, in June 2000 after his arrest on assault and weapons charges.

Eminem had always had issues with his temper. He acknowledges that his mood swings are powerful and even violent. "I could be in a good mood . . . then somebody could just say the wrong [thing] to me, and before you knew it there was nothing my bodyguards could do to stop me from reacting and at least punching, spitting, or kicking a few times before they could get to me," he once wrote. "It would be the simplest [thing] that would set me off, like somebody looking at me hard."[47]

Eminem's Tattoos

Many of Eminem's tattoos reflect the people who are most important in his life. On Eminem's upper left arm is a tattoo that honors Ronnie Pilkington, his uncle who had introduced Eminem to rap. Pilkington's 1991 suicide devastated Eminem.

Among Eminem's many tattoos is a portrait of his daughter on his right shoulder.

Eminem had the name "Hailie Jade" tattooed on the back of his right forearm after his daughter was born. He later had a portrait of her face tattooed on his upper right shoulder and arm, along with the words "Bonnie and Clyde"—from the song on his first album that had featured Hailie's voice. This tattoo covered one that used to read "Eminem." On his left lower arm, Eminem has a large "D" tattooed, to match the number "12" on the lower right arm. Together, the two tattoos read "D12," the name of the Detroit rap group Eminem is part of.

Finally, in the center of Eminem's belly there is an elaborate tattoo of an open grave with the words, "Kim: Rot in Pieces." Eminem got this tattoo in 2001 after he and Kim had a bad fight; he was sure they would not get back together.

His temper affected Eminem's family. Always tumultuous, Eminem's relationship with Scott was in crisis less than a year into their marriage. The sudden fame, Eminem's tours and behavior, including the constant replay and performance of his song

"97 Bonnie and Clyde" in which Kim's fictional dead body was dumped in a lake, strained the couple's already volatile relationship. There were arguments and accusations of cheating on both sides. The discord culminated in June 2000, when Eminem and a friend went to a nightclub parking lot where they thought Scott might be with another guy. When Eminem saw a man kissing his wife, he pistol-whipped him, earning Eminem an arrest and felony charge for carrying a concealed weapon and for assault.

The same week, Eminem was also arrested during an altercation in which he pulled out a gun and threatened a member of the Insane Clown Posse, a Detroit rap group with whom Eminem feuds and whom he puts down in his lyrics. The proximity of these two arrests, along with his aggressive lyrics, earned Eminem a reputation as an angry, violent man.

Divorce Drama

The drama did not end with Eminem's arrests. During the summer of 2000, Eminem headlined the Up in Smoke tour, performing raps from *Slim Shady*, including the infamous "97 Bonnie and Clyde." He put his anger with his wife on full display, often referring to the inflatable doll he kicked around on stage as "Kim." The night Eminem performed in Detroit, Scott slashed her wrists in a suicide attempt. She later blamed the suicide attempt in part on her husband's portrayal of her in his songs and performances. "He's supposed to be the man that loves me and protects me," she said, "and here he is completely and totally disrespecting me in the worst possible way in front of millions of people. And in front of our kids, my family, my friends."[48]

Once Scott recovered, Eminem filed for divorce on August 16, 2000. Less than a week later, Scott filed a $10 million lawsuit against her husband for intentional infliction of emotional distress and sought legal custody of Hailie. The legal back-and-forth between Eminem and Scott lasted nearly a year. The proceedings of the divorce were hard on Eminem. "I would rather have a baby through my penis than get married again," he said after the divorce was finalized. "I can't take what I went through last year. I don't ever want to experience that again."[49]

Eminem attends his sentencing on weapons charges in a Mt. Clemens, Michigan, courtroom in April 2001. The rapper received a total of three years probation and was ordered to take anger management classes stemming from his arrests the previous year.

Scott wasn't the only one who kept Eminem before a judge. During this time, Eminem was in and out of courts with his mother, for his arrests, for a lawsuit brought by De'Angelo Bailey for lyrics about the childhood bully, for another lawsuit filed by the man he had assaulted in June, as well as a suit from a classical jazz pianist who claimed Eminem had sampled his music without permission. In February 2001, Eminem pleaded guilty to the concealed weapon charge, and in March, he pleaded no contest to the charges involving the Insane Clown Posse. As a result, he received a total of three years of probation and was required to take anger management classes. All other suits were either dismissed or settled out of court. It was a hectic, trying time for Eminem.

Dad Duty

During and after his three-year probation, Eminem increasingly took over all parenting responsibilities for Hailie. After the divorce, Kim Scott had had some trouble with the law. She was arrested for drugs and ordered to a rehab program, which she left against court orders. She was placed on house arrest but cut off her ankle tether and went on the run from the police. With Hailie's mother in crisis, Eminem assumed responsibility for the child.

Eminem also took on full custody of Kim's sister's daughter, Alaina, whom he and Scott had cared for on and off since her birth. Alaina had also spent time in the foster care system, bouncing from foster home to foster home. Eminem also watched his younger half brother, Nathan, bounce between foster homes when the courts removed him from Debbie Nelson's care. The familial dysfunction broke Eminem's heart. He had always said that if he could get enough money to provide stability for these children, he would do what he could to provide for them, and now he had that chance.

Eminem became focused on being a good father. He put movie offers on hold and made sure recordings took place in Detroit, so he could be near his family full-time. In addition to staying close to home, Eminem consciously made other changes once his

Kim Mathers stands with her attorney before a judge in a Warren, Michigan, courtroom to face charges of disturbing the peace in 2001. Kim's problems with drugs and the law prompted Eminem to assume all parenting responsibilities for their daughter.

three-year probation was up. "When I got off probation I remember sayin' to myself, 'I'm never [messin'] up again. I'm-a-learn to turn the other cheek.' I took on boxing just to get the stress out. Plus I chilled out a lot as far as the drinking and the drugs and all that stuff."[50] Eminem had always been uncomfortable with the limelight, anyway. He disliked the Los Angeles scene and was not interested in moving there. Sticking close to home and building himself a studio in Detroit was therefore a natural choice for him. It also helped give his kids a normal, stable childhood, as well as helping to keep Eminem on track. Paul Rosenburg, Eminem's friend and manager said, "[Eminem is] amazingly resilient. Most people who have gone through what he's gone through would probably be in a straightjacket. He's been through some serious, serious [stuff]. The relationship with his daughter is what centers him—if he didn't have his daughter, I don't know what would have happened to him."[51]

A couple of years down the road, Eminem added another child to his house. He eventually took custody of Kim's daughter from a different relationship, Whitney. Whitney was Hailie's younger half sister, making Eminem the father of three girls.

Trouble with Drugs

Before Eminem made it big, he had turned to drugs and alcohol to cope when life got hard. After becoming famous, he began using drugs even more regularly. Although Eminem was not an everyday drug user, drugs definitely played a prominent role in his life. Eminem made no secret of his habit: while on tour in 2000, for example, he called into an interview supposedly high on psychedelic mushrooms and even bought drugs while in the company of a *Rolling Stone* reporter.

Getting high became a way that Eminem got into character to perform. Drugs also helped soften the anxiety of performing in front of thousands of fans. He also found it difficult to resist drugs when they were part and parcel of being famous. "The bigger the shows got, the bigger the afterparties," he says. "Drugs were always around. In the beginning it was recreational. I could come off tour and be able to shut it off. I'd spend time with the kids, and I'd be OK."[52]

Eminem became more dependent on drugs in 2001. He was very busy that year, trying to balance rehearsing and filming for *8 Mile* with writing new lyrics, recording new music, and taking care of his daughters. He would sometimes spend sixteen hours on the set and only have a small window of time to get sleep. One day, someone gave him a sleeping pill that helped him go immediately to sleep. Eminem got a prescription and began

Feuds with Other Artists

Eminem's music is full of verbal insults toward others. Indeed, he often instigates ongoing feuds with other artists, known in hip-hop as "beef." Eminem has had an ongoing feud with the Insane Clown Posse. They traded insults on recorded songs before Eminem was arrested for pulling a gun on them in a parking lot. Eminem has also feuded with Ray "Benzino" Scott, the co-owner

The members of the Insane Clown Posse are among several artists and celebrities with whom Eminem has traded public insults.

of the *Source,* a well-known hip-hop magazine. Benzino provoked Eminem by calling him the "Rap Hitler" and accusing him of stealing the culture of rap by being a successful white rapper. Eminem responded in lyric, but the feud fizzled when many began to suspect that Benzino was simply going after Eminem to gain publicity for his own lackluster career and magazine.

Eminem also feuds with other celebrities, especially those who criticize him. He has taken aim at boy bands, Michael Jackson, Christina Aguilera, and Mariah Carey, to name just a few. Eminem has said he thrives on the conflict. "I like it when people [insult me]. Because if people weren't [insulting me], there would be nothing for me to come back with," he once said. "I need that. If I don't have ammo, what am I going to say?"

Quoted in Brian Mockenhaupt. "Eminem, Yeager. " *Esquire,* January 2009.

taking the pills all the time. After several months, he had built up a tolerance to them and had to use more and more to get the same effect. Because he was still on probation, he was required to be drug tested and so was careful to take only what he was legally prescribed. When his probation ended, however, his sleeping pill addiction led him to abuse other substances. "The reins came off," he says. "I was [messed] up every night."[53]

"This Could Be the Final Thing"

Eminem tried to limit drug use to his tours, when he was away from his kids, but soon this too became impossible. Even at home, Eminem began abusing Vicodin and Valium, highly addictive prescription medicines intended to help reduce pain and anxiety. After a while he was taking dozens of pills a day just to feel normal.

By August 2005, Eminem's drug use was so bad, he had to cancel the European leg of his Anger Management tour. At first it was said the cancellation was due to exhaustion, but soon the truth came out: Eminem was addicted to sleeping pills and was leaving the tour to enter a drug rehabilitation program.

A few months later, Aftermath Records released *Curtain Call: The Hits,* a compilation of Eminem's most popular songs as well as four additional tracks. The album cover depicts the close of a curtain with roses thrown onstage, evoking the scene at the end of a show. Many speculated the cover meant Eminem was ending his music career. Eminem only fueled such speculation when he told a Detroit radio station, "I'm at a point in my life right now where I feel like I don't know where my career is going. This is the reason that we called (the new CD) *Curtain Call,* because this could be the final thing. We don't know."[54] Many held their breath hoping that the world would hear more from Slim Shady.

Rehab was a terrible experience for him; it made him feel like a freak on display. "When Bugs Bunny walks into rehab," he once told an interviewer, "people are going to turn and look. People at rehab were stealing my hats and pens and notebooks and asking for autographs. I couldn't concentrate on my problem."[55]

"I Was a Terrible Person"

When he got sober, Eminem left rehab and rekindled his relationship with Kim Scott. Despite their tumultuous past and their 2001 divorce, he asked her to marry him again, and they tied the knot for a second time in January 2006. The wedding this time was larger, held in Michigan, and attended by family and friends such as Dr. Dre, Obie Trice, and 50 Cent. Proof was Eminem's best man. Photographers congregated outside, and news helicopters flew overhead attempting to get a shot.

The couple's second attempt at matrimony was short-lived, however. Less than three months into their second marriage, Eminem filed for divorce, on April 5, 2006. Scott blamed the couple's troubles on Eminem, saying he was still addicted to sleeping pills and possibly cheating on her. Other than denying all of Kim's claims, Eminem refused to release any public statements about their marriage in an effort to protect the children they were raising together.

A week after Eminem filed for divorce, his world caved in when Proof was fatally shot outside a Detroit night club on April 11, 2006. Losing Proof was more than Eminem could bear—he had been Eminem's best friend through thick and thin, the man who pushed him to create Slim Shady. Proof had gone on most of Eminem's tours, had backed him up on stage, and had been the best man at his wedding. "The best way to describe Proof would be a rock," Eminem once said of his friend. "Somebody to confide in, somebody who always had your back. At this point, it's difficult to find people I know I can trust. I still have certain friends like that, but when you lose one, man."[56]

The loss of Proof sent Eminem into a downward spiral. He went into a deep depression. Not even a full year out of rehab, he began using drugs with reckless abandon. Some days were so bad he spent all day in bed crying and taking pills. He gained 80 pounds (36kg) and people began not to recognize him out in public. Most disturbing, he was terrible to friends and family. ""It creeps me out sometimes to think of the person I was. I was a terrible person," he admits. "I was mean to people. I treated people around me [badly]. Obviously I was hiding something.

A program provides details on the funeral services for Proof, who was killed outside a Detroit night club in April 2006. The death of his best friend sent Eminem into a deep depression.

I was [messed] up inside, and people with those kinds of problems tend to put up this false bravado—let me attack everyone else, so the focus is off me. But of course everybody knew."[57]

Two Hours from Death

In December 2007, a couple of days before Christmas and Hailie's twelfth birthday, Eminem accidentally overdosed on methadone. Methadone is a drug that is prescribed to relieve severe pain or to help someone in rehab withdraw from hard drugs such as heroin. If a person takes too much methadone, it slows breathing and causes an irregular heartbeat, both of which are life-threatening. Eminem did not even know he was taking methadone. He had gone to a guy looking for more Vicodin and was given methadone, which looks similar. After taking too many pills, he woke up in the hospital. He had been unconscious for two days. The doctors said when he was brought in, his kidneys were shutting down, and he was less than two hours from death.

After a week in the hospital, Eminem checked himself out, against his doctors' advice. As he tried to kick his habit, he fell down and tore his knee muscle, which required surgery. After the surgery, he suffered from withdrawal from the drugs his body had been used to and had a seizure. After being hospitalized for this, Eminem relapsed completely. "Within a month [my drug use] had ramped right back to where it was before," he said. "That's what really freaked me out. That's when I knew: I either get help, or I am going to die. As a father, I want to be here for things. I don't want to miss anything else."[58]

Going to rehab had not worked for Eminem the first time, so this time he tried a different approach. After detoxing in a hospital, he tried attending meetings but grew frustrated when people doted on his celebrity. He could not simply be an anonymous individual trying to beat addiction. So he got a private rehab counselor whom he continues to see once a week. He also took up running and after a while was running almost 17 miles (27km) a day. Exercise helped relieve some of the anxiety and stress, for relief from which he had always depended on drugs. Finally, he talked to others who had struggled with addiction, such as Elton John. John successfully conquered his own addiction to drugs and alcohol at the height of his fame. John now calls Eminem regularly to check in with the rapper and talk about the journey of staying clean.

During 2006–2008, while Eminem dealt with his addiction, he dropped out of the spotlight. He recorded no albums, was rarely seen in public outside of Detroit, and for a time was not even producing other artists. Even a hiatus of a year is significant in popular music. When Eminem was not heard from for longer, music critics and fans began to suspect that his personal problems had become so large that he would not be returning to the spotlight. It was rumored that Eminem's career was over.

Chapter 5

A Leader in Hip Hop

The world heard little from Eminem between 2005 and 2008. He used his hiatus from recording and performing to battle drug addiction and cope with the depression he suffered after Proof's death. He also took time to realign his priorities. His daughters and making music are the two things Eminem has always loved most. By refocusing on these two things, a clean and sober Eminem was ready in 2008 to pick up his musical career where he had left it.

Rehab and Refocus

As Eminem recovered from drug addition, he found there were many events he had no memory of. He watched videos of himself giving interviews, presentations, and performances, none of which he recollected. "The pills had a lot to do with it," he said. "Just wiping out brain cells. I don't know if it sounds like I'm making excuses, but the absolute truth is a lot of my memory is gone."[59]

Once Eminem was clean, he found he even had to relearn how to rap. He had to learn how to say his lyrics again, how to structure rhymes and make them flow. "When I got clean and sober, it was like I was a kid again," he said. "Everything was new. Not to sound corny, [but] I felt like I was born again. I had to learn my writing skills. I was relearning how to rap. I didn't know if my MC skills were intact. But everything was fun and suddenly I started feeling happy. I hadn't felt happy for a long time."[60]

Eminem the Illustrator

Eminem has been a serious comic-book fan since childhood. Other than LL Cool J's biography and the dictionary, comic books are the only books he has ever read cover to cover.

Eminem is a talented sketch artist. In high school, he often made extra money by decorating clothing for friends with drawings. He even once considered pursuing a career in comics. He has settled for just being a fan, though, and keeps a huge comic book collection. One of his Shady Records executives once said, "Eminem's collection is otherworldly. [He has items that] aren't even on display at the stores."

During his second attempt at rehab, a doctor told him to do unstressful things that he enjoyed while in the hospital. Eminem chose to draw. When preparing to release his comeback album, *Relapse,* Eminem partnered with Marvel Comics to feature himself in a comic book with one of his favorite comic characters, the Punisher.

Quoted in Steven Roberts. "Eminem's Comic-Book Collection Is Otherworldly, Shady Exec Says." MTV.com, December 18, 2009.

In addition to getting excited about music again, the time away from the spotlight helped Eminem determine exactly the kind of father he wanted to be. While Eminem had always been clear that his daughters were his top priority, he had not been living that priority. His overdose made him realize that his drug addiction could very likely kill him and leave his children without a father. This idea hit particularly close to home because Eminem's father had abandoned him. Eminem wanted to do everything in his power to give his kids the childhood he had never had.

The new 15,000-square-foot home (1,394 sq m) that Eminem and his daughters moved into outside of Detroit—which had formerly belonged to the chief executive officer of Kmart—had, among many other things, a recording studio in the basement.

This allowed Eminem to begin recording again in his own basement and still be home for his girls on evenings and weekends. "Makes it very easy for me. I just go downstairs. I'm super relaxed. … It's like the old days, only there's a lot more than a rusty four-track in my basement."[61] Eminem began doing "mind exercises" to get himself writing again and began rapping in the basement studio in preparation for a comeback album. Once he got his lyrical legs back under him, Eminem met Dr. Dre in Orlando, Florida, to begin recording a new album.

The Way I Am

While Eminem was beginning to record, he was also trying his hand at writing. In October 2008, he released a large, photo-filled coffee-table book titled *The Way I Am*. Published by Dutton, the book's title is the name of his favorite song on *Marshall Mathers*. In the song, Eminem bucks everyone's expectations of him. Eminem intended the book to be part-scrapbook for his fans and part memoir. In addition to eight chapters of writing, it features pages of actual lyric sheets in Eminem's signature tiny scrawl. It also showcases candid photos from his years of performing and his own sketches. The eight chapters are full of memories from his childhood, the early days of rapping in Detroit, and his philosophy on parenting his daughters. The book is dedicated to Proof, and a pages-long inscription reveals the depression Eminem fell into after his friend's death.

The memoir provided a rare look into Eminem's life, providing little-known details about the rapper. For instance, Eminem revealed that Slim Shady's dyed blonde hair was an unintentional result of an Ecstasy high and a bottle of peroxide. Eminem also wrote candidly about his three daughters and his life at home. Some reviewers and fans, however, were disappointed that he skimmed over some of the biggest headlines of his life. As Andy Greene of *Rolling Stone* wrote of the memoir, "Eminem largely ignores his ex-wife, Kim, and his litigious mother, Debbie. And the sleeping-pill dependency that landed him in rehab is referred to obliquely."[62]

A poster promoting the memoir Eminem: The Way I Am *is displayed at a book release party in New York City in October 2008.*

Nonetheless, the memoir reconnected Eminem with his fan base and cultivated buzz for his upcoming new music release. Perhaps more important than any of its revelations, Eminem's book was a way for him to reenter the music scene before his album did. It reminded people who he was—an underdog who had made it, an equal opportunity offender, and a devoted dad— why they loved him, and why they might anxiously await his next album.

Relapse

On May 19, 2009, Eminem released *Relapse*, his sixth studio album. The album marked the end of his five-year hiatus from recording. Eminem and Dre worked at such a feverish pace on the album that they recorded hundreds of tracks and had enough finished songs to make three new albums. Eminem attributes the productivity to his sobriety. "The deeper I got into my addiction, the tighter the lid on my creativity," he explained. "When I got sober the lid just came off. In seven months I accomplished more than I could accomplish in three or four years of doing drugs."[63]

Eminem and Dr. Dre thought hard about how Eminem should reenter the music world. In the end, they both agreed that the world wanted more Slim Shady. As a result, *Relapse* presented the familiar pattern of violence, celebrity mocking, multiple person-alities, and a blur between the truth of Eminem's life and fiction. Several of the songs concerned his drug rehabilitation, and the album followed a fictional relapse into drug use. The album cover reflected this; it is a portrait of Eminem created from different colored pills. The album title is made to look like a prescription label, with the name of the prescribing physician shown as "Dr. Dre." The album debuted number one on the *Billboard* 200 chart the week it was released and was the biggest release of the year, with sales of 608,000 albums in just the first week.

Reflecting its commercial reception, *Relapse* won two Grammys, including Best Rap Album. However, music critics and fans gave the album mixed reviews. A few critics lauded the complex rhymes and the depth of material that was clearly based on Eminem's personal problems. But others album criticized it

Eminem performs at the 2010 Grammy Awards, at which Relapse *was named Best Rap Album.*

for not tackling new territory and for taking the old Slim Shady shtick too far. As music critic Robert Christagau said of the album, "Rape, murder, drugs and unspeakable combinations of the three abound. You don't have to believe he's advocating anything to find the casual, almost ingrained misogyny here, hurtful, distasteful and dangerous, the way his deeply felt private obsessions never were."[64] Eminem admitted the album had issues. "I wasn't disappointed when I put it out," he said. "The further I got away from *Relapse*, I was able to hear the problems … and how the serial killing didn't work. The joke was over—I ran it into the ground."[65]

From *Relapse to Recovery*

Eminem had intended to release a second *Relapse* album during 2009 to showcase the full range of songs he and Dre had recorded during their Orlando and Detroit sessions; however, he kept pushing the release of the second album back as he recorded more songs and branched out to work with new producers. The result was that he rereleased the album at the end of 2009 with a few additional songs, calling it *Relapse: Refill*, to tide over his fans while he continued to experiment with new songs. Eminem ultimately scrapped all the songs he and Dre had recorded during his feverish post-rehab recording sessions. "*Relapse* was a lot of me relearning how to rap again, since I was doing it for the first time in so long being sober. I was more concerned with the act of rapping and still maintaining my 'bugged out' subject matter. Because of that, I think I lost [the] focus of the actual songs."[66]

The new material Eminem recorded was more focused and honest; he recognized that he was moving beyond the "jokes." The new album was named *Recovery*. It was released on June 15, 2010. For this album, Eminem worked with Dr. Dre and several new producers, including Just Blaze, Boi 1da, Alex the Kid, and Denaun Porter ("Kon Artis" of D12). Eminem also recorded in a number of different studios, in Detroit as well as in Hawaii and London, among other places. Of this change, Eminem said, "It was just time for fresh blood."[67]

In addition to partnering with new producers, this album featured guest appearances from solo singers Rihanna and Pink, but only one guest rapper, Lil Wayne. Nearly all of his past records had featured members of his D12 group and/or rappers signed to Eminem's Shady label. Lil Wayne was not related to Slim Shady in either of these ways but was a chart-topping rap artist and producer in his own right.

Fierce and Focused

Fans and critics agreed that Eminem turned a corner with this new release. They were excited by what they heard. "If Eminem seemed to be losing his footing in recent years, he regains it here with his fiercest and most focused work in a long time," wrote critic Steve Jones. "The differences in tone and attitude are evident. He aims for substance over shock value, vividly spilling out details of his various tribulations. Gone are the wacky skits and goofy foreign accents."[68] For Eminem, there was enough distance from his drug troubles that he could rap about them on this album, making it more honest than the last. "I've never really

Eminem appears with pop singer Rihanna, left, in the video for "Love the Way You Lie," their collaboration from his Recovery *album, released in 2010.*

been shy about expressing my feelings. It's always about timing with me, like, 'When am I ready to talk about this or that?'" he said. "Right now I think I've resolved a lot of my issues."[69] Reflecting this feeling, the album was more upbeat than others. In the song, "Not Afraid," for example, Eminem offers a hand to those who are immersed in their own dark days, be they the result of drugs or something else.

The response to *Recovery* was fantastic. It debuted, like many of his other albums, at the number one spot on the *Billboard* chart. The albums sales were strong out of the gate and the album continued to sell well all through the year. It was the first album in history to sell a million digital downloads. Several of the singles on the album received remarkable playtime. "Not Afraid" was the first single released; it debuted on the *Billboard* Hot 100, a weekly list of the hundred most popular songs in America. It is unusual for a debuting song to make this list until it has been out and heard for at least a week. "Not Afraid" was only the seventeenth song in *Billboard*'s history and the second rap song ever to debut on the Hot 100 list. "Love the Way You Lie" was the second single of the album and features Rihanna singing opposite Eminem's rapping in a fictional abusive relationship. This song was so popular that it stayed on the Hot 100 list for seven consecutive weeks and more than a year later was still in active play at most pop and hip-hop stations.

Back on Stage and Back on Top

After the release of *Relapse,* Eminem slowly began making appearances and performing again. The day after *Relapse* was released Eminem held a free concert in Detroit to celebrate. In October 2009, Eminem performed at the Voodoo Music Experience as a headlining artist. It was his first full-length performance since returning to the spotlight. After the release of *Recovery,* however, Eminem's comeback was truly solid, and people began to clamor for performances.

Eminem and Jay-Z, right, perform together at Detroit's Comerica Park in September 2010 on a mini-tour that also included shows at New York's Yankee Stadium.

Eminem's Return to the Stage

The day after Eminem released *Relapse* he returned to the stage for the first time since recovering from his drug problem. He performed a free concert in Detroit's Motor City Hotel to celebrate the release of his comeback album. Prior to the forty-minute performance, Eminem provided free tickets to the event that his fans had to find in a citywide scavenger hunt. Eminem provided clues one at time from his Twitter account. Some of the clues were, "Ok, Paul has a pair of tix at the Original Pancake House on Woodward and 14 Mile. He's hungry, so come quick," and "A man with a mohawk named Andrew is standing in front of Comerica Park at the Tiger. He has four tickets."

Eminem performs a free concert at Detroit's Motor City Casino to promote the release of Relapse.

Once on stage Eminem asked the crowd, "Detroit, did you miss me?" He then performed seven songs from the new album as well as his famous, "Lose Yourself," for which the entire D12 group joined him on stage. In addition to celebrating his return on stage, Eminem also gave tribute to Proof, the D12 member and close friend who had died in a shooting while Eminem was out of the spotlight. The show was also significant because it was one of Eminem's first shows he performed entirely sober. "This is one of the best shows I've probably ever done, because when I get off stage, I'm actually going to remember it."

Quoted in Daniel Kreps. "Eminem Honors Proof at Free *Relapse* Show in Detroit." *Rolling Stone,* May 20, 2009.

In the summer of 2010, Eminem planned a mini-tour with Jay-Z. Originally they only planned two shows, one in Eminem's Detroit and the other in Jay-Z's hometown of New York. After those concerts quickly sold out, they added an additional date in each city. A clean and sober Eminem pulled off an exciting show for his fans. "Em proved he still has that rare connection with his fanbase," wrote one reporter. "Grown men took off their shirts and got rock-n-roll rowdy when he rapped. It was clear that Em missed his fans as well. He was engaging, lively and energetic on this night."[70]

The King of Hip Hop

By the time 2010 drew to a close, Eminem had received numerous affirmations from fans and the music industry. BET (Black Entertainment Television) named him the number one rapper of the twenty-first century. MTV honored him as the 2010 "Hottest MC in the Game." Interviewers were again knocking on his door. The popular TV newsmagazine *60 minutes* did a special on Eminem, sending correspondent Anderson Cooper to walk the streets of Detroit with Eminem in order to bring his story to a mainstream news audience.

In addition, by year's end *Recovery* was the most popular and best-selling album of 2010. In the Grammy Awards that followed, Eminem received the Grammy for Best Rap Album for *Recovery,* as well as the Grammy for Best Rap Solo for his song "Not Afraid."

Eminem was back on top, and just two years after he had reentered the music scene. In fact, he was so popular, that *Rolling Stone* officially crowned him the "King of Hip Hop" in 2011. The magazine used album sales, chart rankings, YouTube video views, social media numbers, concert ticket sales, industry awards, and critic ratings to measure and rank twenty different artists during the period from January 2009 to November 2010. Despite the fact that the world had not heard from Eminem for several years when the data for the *Rolling Stone* article began to be collected, Eminem still earned the reigning title. His record sales were more than two and a half times that of any other rapper of the period.

Eminem accepts the award for Best Rap Album for Recovery at the 2011 Grammy Awards, where he also won Best Rap Solo for the song "Not Afraid."

Eminem also ruled the online world. With 1.3 billion views of his music videos as of November 2011, he had the most total video views on YouTube of the rappers, beating the others because of the popularity of not one, but two videos from *Recovery* (for "Not Afraid" and "Love the Way You Lie"). In addition, in 2010, Eminem was the most "liked" thing on Facebook, other than Facebook itself. With more than 49 million Facebook fans, Eminem had more "likes" than even top artists outside of rap, such as Lady Gaga.

"My Biggest Accomplishment"

Eminem was careful to balance his comeback success with his family responsibilities. "With drugs I knew I'd let my kids down," he said. "I thought, 'What if they looked at me like I was Superman and all I ever do is disappoint them?'"[71] Now clean, Eminem focuses on being there and providing stability and protection for his kids. He helps with homework, though admits it can be difficult for him since he never passed ninth grade. He forbids the use of profanity in his house. He is setting expectations that his daughters will go to college.

Eminem is especially protective of his children's privacy. For example, he doesn't allow the media to take photographs of the girls. Eminem was unprepared for the way fame changed his life, and he wants his daughters to be sheltered from the parts of fame he despises, such as not being able to go out in public without an entourage and losing personal privacy. He wants to give his girls a regular childhood and allow them to function as normally as possible despite his fame. This is also one of the reasons he has stayed in Detroit: because it is his children's hometown. Detroit is where they are comfortable, and Eminem wants to offer them the stability he lacked. "I want my girls to have a place where they belong and feel protected," he wrote in his book. "That's why I say my biggest accomplishment is being a father."[72]

Going forward, Eminem says he wants to make up for the years he stepped back from his career. He plans to keep rapping and producing as long as it feels right. He also says he would consider doing another film. Eminem is clear, however, that whereas music

Bad Meets Evil

Back in the game, Eminem continued to cultivate artists through his Shady Records label. By 2011 Eminem had several new artists, including Slaughterhouse and Yelawolf, as well as a new collaboration called Bad Meets Evil. Bad Meets Evil is made up of Royce da 5'9" (Bad) and Eminem (Evil). The two were intertwined in a beef for years but reconciled after Proof's death and began anew by recording songs together.

In June 2011, Bad Meets Evil released *Hell: The Sequel*. The album sold 171,000 copies its first week, making it the top debuting album of the week. With the success of *Hell: The Sequel*, Eminem became the first artist in several years to have had two best-selling records released in the same twelve-month period.

is his passion, his family will always be his priority. "My dad role is more important than my *8 Mile* role or my emcee role. But I'll never forget about the mic," he says. "Hailie's daddy is still a better rapper than your daddy."[73]

As of 2012, Hailie's daddy was indeed a better rapper than most, and Eminem's rap career had broken all records for what successful rappers can achieve. Even before his hiatus, Eminem was credited with bringing rap to the mainstream. Now, back on top, the King of Hip-Hop is continuing to build his legacy as an artist who enjoys keeping everyone talking. His passion for music is no less diminished than it was ten years ago. "The only thing that is not a joke," Eminem says, "is the passion I have for emceeing. It's the foundation of what makes me so 'talked about.' I take it extremely seriously. It's how I express myself creatively. Whether during good times, bad times, or even the worst of times, I've used the pen to express myself."[74] With Eminem focused again on his music, the world is waiting for what he will come up with next.

Notes

Introduction: The Underdog Takes the Stage

1. Jon Caramanica. "Eminem Reasserts His Core Values." *New York Times,* June 21, 2010. www.nytimes.com/2010/06/22/ arts/music/22eminem.html?ref=eminem.
2. Quoted in Josh Eells. "Eminem: The Road Back from Hell." *Rolling Stone,* October 17, 2011. www.rollingstone.com/music/ news/eminem-on-the-road-back-from-hell-20111017.

Chapter 1: Instability and Hardship

3. Quoted in Charles Aaron. "Chocolate on the Inside." *Spin Magazine,* May 1999.
4. Eminem. *The Way I Am.* New York: Dutton, 2008, p. 141.
5. Quoted in Aaron. "Chocolate on the Inside."
6. Eminem. *The Way I Am,* pp. 20–21.
7. Quoted in Anthony Bozza. "Eminem Blows Up." *Rolling Stone,* April 29, 1999. www.rollingstone.com/music/news/eminem-blows-up-20091105.
8. Quoted in Lisa Robinson. "Eminem's World." *Vanity Fair,* December 2004.
9. Quoted in Bozza. "Eminem Blows Up."
10. Eminem. *The Way I Am,* p. 134.
11. Quoted in TOURÃ©. "Eminem." *Rolling Stone,* November 25, 2004.
12. Quoted in Bozza. "Eminem Blows Up."
13. Quoted in Bozza. "Eminem Blows Up."
14. Quoted in Neva Chonin. "Rage Against the Past; Eminem Is a Former Skinny Kid Who Raps with a Vengeance." *San Francisco Chronicle,* May 8, 1999. http://articles.sfgate. com/1999-05-08/entertainment/17686622_1_marshall-mathers-slim-shady-lp-eminem.

Chapter 2: The Road to Success

15. Eminem. *The Way I Am,* p. 22.
16. Quoted in Robinson. "Eminem's World."
17. Eminem. *The Way I Am,* p. 26.

18. Eminem. *The Way I Am,* p. 23.
19. Quoted in Anthony Bozza. *Whatever You Say I Am: The Life and Times of Eminem.* New York: Crown, 2003, p. 19.
20. Eminem. *The Way I Am,* p. 32.
21. Quoted in Bozza. *Whatever You Say I Am,* p. 22.
22. Quoted in Bozza. *Whatever You Say I Am,* p. 22–23.
23. Quoted in Damien Cave et al. "The Birth of Slim Shady." *Rolling Stone,* June 24, 2004.
24. Quoted in Cave et al. "The Birth of Slim Shady."
25. Bozza. "Eminem Blows Up."
26. Quoted in Bozza. *Whatever You Say I Am,* p. 52.

Chapter 3: A Controversial Artist

27. Neil Strauss. "Eminem Enters 'N Sync Turf." *New York Times,* June 7, 2000. www.nytimes.com/2000/06/07/arts/the-pop-life-eminem-enters-n-sync-turf.html?pagewanted=all&src=pm.
28. Quoted in Anthony DeCurtis. "Eminem's Hate Rhymes." *Rolling Stone,* August 3, 2000.
29. Eminem. *The Way I Am,* p. 54.
30. Quoted in A.D. "Eminem Responds." *Rolling Stone,* August 3, 2000.
31. Quoted in CNN.com. "Lynne Cheney Discusses Hollywood Violence; Bill Bradley Talks Presidential Politics; What Role Will Gender Gap Play in Election?" Transcript, September 17, 2000. http://edition.cnn.com/TRANSCRIPTS/0009/17/le.00.html.
32. Quoted in Robinson. "Eminem's World."
33. Quoted in Zadie Smith. "If a Man Picks Up a Microphone, That's It You See?" *Daily Telegraph* (London), January 13, 2003.
34. DeCurtis. "Eminem's Hate Rhymes."
35. Quoted in Robinson. "Eminem's World."
36. Quoted in David Segal. "A Bum Rap? Eminem's Grammy Nominations Ignite Protests by Gay-Rights Groups, Parents." *Chicago Tribune,* January 8, 2001. http://articles.chicagotribune.com/2001-01-08/features/0101080168_1_naras-eminem-marshall-mathers-lp.
37. Madonna. "In Defense of a Fellow Artist." *Los Angeles Times,* February 18, 2001. http://articles.latimes.com/2001/feb/18/entertainment/ca-26775.
38. Elton John. "Eminem." *Rolling Stone,* April 21, 2005.

39. Robert Wilonsky. "The Eminem Show Aftermath." *Miami New Times,* June 20, 2002. www.miaminewtimes.com/2002-06-20/music/eminem/.

40. Neva Chonin. "With 'Encore,' Eminem Proves He Isn't Ready to Grow Up, at Least Not Yet." *San Francisco Chronicle,* November 15, 2004. http://articles.sfgate.com/2004-11-15/entertainment/17451639_1_eminem-encore-mix-tape-toy-soldiers.

41. Quoted in Robinson. "Eminem's World."

42. Sasha Frere-Jones. "Fifth Grade: Eminem's Growing Pains." *New Yorker,* December 6, 2004. www.newyorker.com/archive/2004/12/06/041206crmu_music#ixzz1a9MyjbPM.

Chapter 4: Downward Spiral

43. Quoted in N'Gai Croal. "Slim Shady Sounds Off." *Newsweek,* May 29, 2000.

44. Anderson Cooper. "Eminem's Incredible Rise to Stardom." *60 Minutes,* transcript, August 7, 2011. www.cbsnews.com/stories/2010/10/07/60minutes/main6936406.shtml.

45. Quoted in Croal. "Slim Shady Sounds Off."

46. Quoted in Deborah Solomon. "The Real Marshall Mathers." *New York Times,* June 16, 2010. www.nytimes.com/2010/06/20/magazine/20fob-q4-t.html.

47. Eminem. *The Way I Am,* p. 130.

48. Quoted in Susan Whitall. "Em and Kim: A Timeline." *Detroit News,* February 17, 2007. http://detnews.com/article/20070217/ENT01/702170396/Em-and-Kim--A-tumultuous-10-year-timeline.

49. Quoted in Anthony Bozza. "The Rolling Stone Interview: Eminem." *Rolling Stone,* July 4, 2002.

50. Quoted in TOURÃ©. "The *Rolling Stone* Interview: Eminem."

51. Quoted in Robinson. "Eminem's World."

52. Quoted in Eells. "Eminem: The Road Back from Hell."

53. Quoted in Eells. "Eminem: The Road Back from Hell."

54. Quoted in "Eminem Remarries Ex-wife Kimberly." *People Weekly,* January 16, 2006. www.people.com/people/article/0,,1147983,00.html.

55. Quoted in Solomon. "Questions for Eminem: The Real Marshall Mathers."
56. Quoted in Eells. "Eminem: The Road Back from Hell."
57. Quoted in Eells. "Eminem: The Road Back from Hell."
58. Quoted in Eells. "Eminem: The Road Back from Hell."

Chapter 5: A Leader in Hip-Hop

59. Quoted in Eells. "Eminem: The Road Back From Hell."
60. Quoted in Dan Aquilante. "Eminem: 'I Hated Myself.'" *New York Post,* September 11, 2010. www.nypost.com/f/print/entertainment/music/losing_myself_PT0Nnh4CJfFdcPtsAtQnJK.
61. Eminem. *The Way I Am,* p. 203.
62. Andy Greene. "Slim Shady Breaks His Silence." *Rolling Stone,* October 21, 2008. www.rollingstone.com/music/news/book-review-slim-shady-breaks-his-silence-in-eminem-the-way-i-am-20081021.
63. Quoted in Jon Pareles. "Get Clean, Come Back: Eminem's Return." *New York Times,* May 21, 2009. www.nytimes.com/2009/05/24/arts/music/24pare.html?pagewanted=all.
64. Quoted in Robert Christgau. "Eminem: A 'Relapse' of Horror?" National Public Radio, May 20, 2009. www.npr.org/templates/story/story.php?storyId=104349227.
65. Quoted in Aquilante. "Eminem: 'I Hated Myself.'"
66. Quoted in Lisa Robinson. "Hot Tracks." *Vanity Fair,* June 2010.
67. Quoted in Eells. "Eminem: The Road Back from Hell."
68. Steve Jones. "Eminem's 'Recovery' Is an Addictive Hip-Hop Comeback." *USA Today,* June 21, 2010. www.usatoday.com/life/music/reviews/2010-06-21-eminemreview21_ST_N.htm.
69. Quoted in Robinson. "Hot Tracks."
70. Shaheem Reid. "Eminem, Jay-Z Joined by Dr. Dre, Drake at Historic Detroit Concert." MTV.com, September 3, 2010. www.mtv.com/news/articles/1647120/eminem-jayz-joined-by-dr-dre-drake-at-historic-detroit-concert.jhtml.
71. Quoted in Aquilante. "Eminem: 'I Hated Myself.'"
72. Eminem. *The Way I Am,* p. 151.
73. Eminem. *The Way I Am,* p. 151.
74. Eminem. *Angry Blonde.* New York: Regan Books, 2000, p. 3.

1972

Marshall B. Mathers III is born on October 17, 1972, in St. Joseph, Missouri. Mathers's father abandons his family before Marshall is a year old.

1992

Funky Bass Team (FBT) Productions signs Eminem (then M&M) to its label.

1995

Daughter, Hailie Jade, is born on December 25, 1995.

1996

First album, *Infinite,* is released by Web Entertainment; changes his stage name from "M&M" to the phonetic spelling "Eminem"; begins competing in battles at Detroit's Hip Hop Shop, at Proof's urging. The Dirty Dozen, or D12 is formed, and Eminem creates the alter-ego Slim Shady.

1997

Participates in the Los Angeles Rap Olympics, taking second place.

1999

The *Slim Shady LP* is released on February 23, 1999. It wins the Grammy for Best Rap Album. Wins Best Solo Rap Performance for his song "My Name Is"; marries Kim Scott on June 14; founds Shady Records and signs D12.

2000

Marshall Mathers is released on May 23, setting a new sales record. The album also wins a Grammy for Best Rap Album and is nominated for Album of the Year. In June, Eminem is arrested twice and charged with assault and carrying a concealed weapon.

2002

Releases *The Eminem Show* album in May; headlines the Anger Management Tour; in November, *8 Mile,* is released. Eminem's original song for the movie soundtrack, "Lose Yourself," is awarded an Oscar.

2004

Releases *Encore,* his fourth studio album on November 12.

2005

Headlines the Anger Management Tour but cancels the European leg to enter rehab for his addiction to sleeping pills.

2006

In January, Eminem and Kim remarry in a lavish ceremony. They divorce less than three months later. In April, DeShaun Holton (Proof) is shot and killed outside a club. Eminem falls into a drug-fueled depression.

2007

In December, overdoses on methadone. Later, hospitalizes himself to detox, then continues the rehab process at home with a private counselor.

2008

Releases memoir, *The Way I Am.*

2009

Releases his sixth studio album, *Relapse,* on May 19. It wins a Grammy for Best Rap Album. Releases *Relapse: Refill* in December.

2010

Releases the album *Recovery* on June 15. *Recovery* earns Eminem his fifth Grammy in the category of Best Rap Album. He also wins a Grammy for his song, "Not Afraid."

2011

Former enemies Eminem and Royce da 5'9 reconcile after Proof's death and collaborate as Bad Meets Evil and release an album, *Hell: The Sequel.*

For More Information

Books

Anthony Bozza. *Whatever You Say I Am: The Life and Times of Eminem*. New York: Crown, 2003. Written by a *Rolling Stone* reporter who covered Eminem during his early career and had unique access to the rapper, often traveling on tour with him, this biography is a highly intimate look at Eminem during his rise to fame.

Eminem. *Angry Blonde*. New York: Regan Books, 2000. This book contains lyrics from Eminem's *Slim Shady* and *Marshall Mathers* albums. In between each set of lyrics, Eminem gives background on where particular lines came from.

Eminem with Sacha Jenkins. *The Way I Am*. New York: Dutton, 2008. This memoir includes memories of growing up, his early rapping career in Detroit's underground scene, and details about his rise to fame. The book contains candid photos of Eminem and real lyrics sheets.

Periodicals

A.D. "Eminem Responds." *Rolling Stone*, August 3, 2000.

Dan Aquilante. "Losing Myself: In an Exclusive Interview Eminem Tells the Post How Pills Took Over His Life and Music." *New York Post*, September 12, 2010.

Anthony Bozza. "Eminem Blows Up." *Rolling Stone*, April 29, 1999.

Anthony Bozza and Lindsay Goldberg. "The *Rolling Stone* Interview: Eminem." *Rolling Stone*, July 4, 2002.

Lisa Robinson. "Eminem's World." *Vanity Fair*, December 2004.

Deborah Solomon. "Questions for Eminem: The Real Marshall Mathers." New York Times, June 16, 2010.

Internet Sources

Anderson Cooper. "Eminem's Incredible Rise to Stardom." *60 Minutes,* transcript, August 7, 2011. www.cbsnews.com/stories/ 2010/10/07/60minutes/main6936406.shtml.

Josh Eells. "Eminem: The Road Back from Hell." *Rolling Stone,* November 25, 2010.

Sasha Frere-Jones. "Fifth Grade: Eminem's Growing Pains." *New Yorker,* December 6, 2004. ww.newyorker.com/archive/2004/ 12/06/041206crmu_music#ixzz1a9MyjbPM.

Chris Molanphy. "Introducing the King of Hip-Hop." *Rolling Stone,* August 15, 2011. www.rollingstone.com/music/news/ introducing-the-king-of-hip-hop-20110815.

Websites

8 Mile (www.8-mile.com/). The official website for the movie has a trailer available and plays music from the movie.

Eminem (www.eminem.com/). Eminem's official website shows videos for his songs as well as Shady Records' signed artists, releases news about Eminem, contains a calendar of events and a forum for fans.

Shade 45 (www.siriusxm.com/shade45). This is the website for Eminem's all-hip-hop satellite radio station. Videos are available of different radio shows that have aired on the channel.

Shady Records (www.shadyrecords.com). This website provides the official news, artist information, tour dates, and downloads for the record label run by Eminem.

Christie Brewer Boyd lives in Ohio with her husband and daughter. She is envious of Eminem's claim that he can find a rhyme for any word.